CATCHING-101

The Complete Guide for Baseball Catchers

by XAN BARKSDALE

AuthorHouse™
1663 Liberty Drive
Bloomington, IN 47403
www.authorhouse.com
Phone: 1-800-839-8640

© 2011 Xan Barksdale. All rights reserved.

No part of this book may be reproduced, stored in a retrieval system, or transmitted by any means without the written permission of the author.

First published by AuthorHouse   7/26/2011

ISBN: 978-1-4634-3961-3 (sc)
ISBN: 978-1-4634-3960-6 (hc)
ISBN: 978-1-4634-3959-0 (e)

Library of Congress Control Number: 2011912493

Printed in the United States of America

Any people depicted in stock imagery provided by Thinkstock are models, and such images are being used for illustrative purposes only. Certain stock imagery © Thinkstock.

This book is printed on acid-free paper.

Because of the dynamic nature of the Internet, any web addresses or links contained in this book may have changed since publication and may no longer be valid. The views expressed in this work are solely those of the author and do not necessarily reflect the views of the publisher, and the publisher hereby disclaims any responsibility for them.

authorHOUSE®

Thank You

This book wouldn't have been possible without the help of many people. I'd like to thank all of the coaches who spent their time teaching me the game of baseball. It is because of them that I have developed a deep love for the greatest game on earth. I'd also like to thank the most important people in my life: my dad, Fountain, my mom, Sandy, and my brother, Andy. Thank you for your love and support. Everything that I have accomplished I owe to you!

Contents

Foreword by Ron Polk ix
Introduction 1
Equipment 5
   Mitt 6
   Face Mask/Helmet 7
   Chest Protector 8
   Supportive Cup 10
   Shin Guards 10
   Catcher's Thumb 11
   Knee Savers 12
   Wristbands/Sweatbands 13
Stances 14
   Signal Stance 14
   Primary Stance 18
   Secondary Stance 19
Receiving 22
   Quiet Body 22
   Strong Hands 23
Blocking 27
   Chest Leaning Slightly Forward 28
   Mitt Covering the Five Hole 29
   Elbows Tucked into Sides 29

    Shoulders Rounded Forward 30
    Chin Tucked in 30
    Falling Forward 31
    Replacing Feet/Knees 31

Throwing to Bases 35
    Arm Strength 35
    Quickness 36
    Accuracy 36
    Throwing to First Base 39
    Throwing to Second Base 42
    Throwing to Third Base 46

Plays at Home Plate 49
    Tag Plays at the Plate 49
    Force Plays at Home Plate 56
    Getting Run Over 58

Pop Flies 60

Fielding Bunts 64
    Bunts to 1B 66
    Bunts Back to the Pitcher 67
    Bunts to 3B 68
    Blocked Third Strikes 69

Pass Balls/Wild Pitches 72
    Field it Like a Bunt 73
    Throw it Like a Dart 74
    Make a Good Throw 74

Pitchouts 76

Intentional Walks 79

Backing up First Base 82

Full Arm Fake 84

Knowing the Field 86
    Backstop 86
    Warning Track 87
    Dugouts 87
    Baselines 87
    Weather 87

Foul Territory 88
Ground Rules 88

Pre-Game Infield/Outfield 89

Giving Catchers Accurate Feedback 91
Video Evaluation 91
Catcher's Performance Summary 93

Communicating with the Umpire 97

Being Vocal on the Field 100

Warming Up Before a Practice or Game 102

Signals 104
Giving Signals 104
Signs with a Runner on Second Base 106
Hot Sign 107
First Sign after the "2" 108
Ahead, Behind, Even 108
Outs + 1 109
Indicator System 109
Pump System 110
Tap System 110

Catching Wristband 112

Catching a Ceremonial First Pitch 115

Catcher's Practice 116

Receiving Drills 118
Receiving Tennis Balls Bare-Handed 118
Partner Throws – Short Distance 119
Partner Throws – Longer Distance 120
Receiving from Pitching Machine 121
Quick Hands Drill 123
Receiving Incrediballs 123
Catching in the Bullpen 124

Blocking Drills 127
Partner Blocking, Straight Ahead 128
Partner Blocking to Both Sides 129
Blocking Balls from a Pitching Machine 130

  Half and Half 130
  Hockey Goalie Drill 132

Throwing Drills 133
  Throwing Standing Up 134
  Throwing from Secondary Stance 134
  Throwing After Receiving a Pitch 134
  Throwing Three-Fourths Distance to Base 135
  Dry Throws on the Foul Line 135

Drills for Catcher Pop Flies 137
  Pop Flies from Fungo 137
  Pop Flies from a Pitching Machine 138
  Fouled off Bunts 138
  Eagle Eye Drill 139

Drills for Plays at Home Plate 140
  Digs – Glove side/Backhand 140
  Balls Hit from Fungo 141
  1, 2, 3 Double Play 142
  Full Arm Fake and Look to 3B 143

Drills for Pass Balls/Wild Pitches 144

Drills for Fielding Bunts 146

Summary 148

Catcher's Dictionary 149

Foreword

I have been very fortunate to have been involved in coaching college baseball for 44 years, and in those years, I have been asked to review many manuscripts, books, videos, tapes, etc. on all aspects of coaching our great game.

When I received Xan Barksdale's book on catching, I started the review process to ensure that it was something I considered worthwhile for coaches and players alike, since my name would be mentioned in support of the publication.

I knew enough about Xan's background as a player in high school, in junior college, at Ole Miss, in professional baseball, and now as a college coach to know that he would have some knowledge of the game of baseball and, in particular, aspects of developing catchers for all levels of competition.

What I didn't know about Xan surprised me. As I started digesting the information contained in his catching book, I was truly amazed at the depth and quality of the information he is passing along to catchers and coaches at all levels of play.

I truly feel that Catching-101 is a book that can help all coaches and players in regards to teaching catching mechanics, drills, and more. It has to be the most comprehensive, readable, and enlightening book on catching that I have ever come across. You would think that I could learn very little on any aspect of the game of baseball since I am going on so many years as a coach at the college level. Well, I learned a lot of technical details on catching that I was not totally aware of.

This is a 'must read book' for coaches and catchers at every level. I encourage you to digest the knowledge, enjoy it, and place it in your library of baseball instructional books. With an entire chapter on catching a ceremonial first pitch, this book definitely covers all aspects of being a catcher.

Thus, I can highly recommend Xan's catching book without hesitation or reservation. As a head coach at Mississippi State University for 29 years, it is not easy for me to endorse a former player at rival Ole Miss as he ventures into the publishing business, since this team rivalry goes way back in time!

But I can endorse this book as a masterpiece of information that can help both coaches and players better understand how to teach and play a highly technical position. Xan Barksdale explains the technical aspects of catching and teaches everyone how to be more successful.

- Ron Polk, ABCA Hall of Fame

Chapter 1

Introduction

Catching, in my opinion, is the most fun position on the baseball field. You're in the action on every play of the game and have a lot to do with your team's success. A good catcher can help a team win games, while a poor catcher can assist in giving away valuable runs. As fun as playing catcher is, it is also probably the most difficult position on the field. Catchers have more skills to master than any other position player; they must be able to receive, block, throw, field bunts and pop flies, handle pass balls and wild pitches, and make plays at the plate, just to name a few!

As exciting as catching can be, it is often overlooked because there is not a lot of quality information about the position. My goal in this book is to provide you with excellent information that will help you better understand catching and will teach you drills and mechanics to help take your game to the next level. This book should be used in conjunction with my website www.Catching-101.com. There are several free videos and articles posted on the website that go hand in hand with the topics covered in this book and they should be viewed to help you understand the drills and mechanics that we will cover. Referencing these videos and articles will help you fully understand every topic covered in this book. I am constantly adding new videos that are related to all aspects of catching, so be sure to check the website often for updates.

CATCHING-101

If you search your local libraries and the Internet, you will find more books on hitting and pitching that anyone could ever read, but you won't find many sources of quality information about catching. I hope to change that situation with this book!

Having played baseball at almost every level, from Little League to professional baseball, I've learned many tips and tricks along the way that I want to share with you. I have been blessed to have had a lot of success playing baseball. Now I find my joy in sharing what I have learned with players who have a thirst for knowledge. I love coaching, but I especially love coaching catchers!

I began my coaching career at the University of Louisville in the fall of 2006 after retiring from a career in professional baseball with the Atlanta Braves. In my first season with the Louisville Cardinals, we finished sixth in the country with the school's first ever trip to the College World Series at Rosenblatt Stadium in Omaha, Nebraska.

I grew up in Madison, Mississippi where I started to develop a love for the game of baseball at the age of four. I played my first season as a catcher when I was seven years old, and that's when my love for catching began. I then continued to play Little League baseball and travel baseball until I began high school.

My high school career was played at Madison-Ridgeland Academy (MRA) from 1997 to 2000. While at MRA, I earned All-Conference honors and was selected as a Mississippi state All-Star. I was also a member of the National Honor Society and graduated with honors in May of 2000.

I then continued my education at Holmes Community College in Goodman, MS while playing baseball for the Bulldogs under coach Kenny Dupont. At HCC I continued to learn the game of baseball while earning an Associate's degree in Engineering in

The Complete Guide for Baseball Catchers

May of 2002. I was also a member of Phi Theta Kappa Honor Society.

After playing at HCC, I pursued my bachelor's degree at the University of Mississippi (Ole Miss) and played for coach Mike Bianco. The Rebels were ranked as high as fourth in the country during my time there, and we hosted the school's first NCAA Regional in 2004. After my senior season, I signed a free agent contract with the Atlanta Braves.

After my first professional season with the Atlanta Braves, I returned to school to complete my bachelor's degree. In May 2005 I was awarded a Business Administration degree from the University of Mississippi, with an emphasis in Marketing and a minor in Math. I was also a member of Phi Sigma Pi National Honor Fraternity.

From 2004 to 2006, I wore a Braves uniform and spent time playing in the Gulf Coast League, Appalachian League, South Atlantic League, and the Carolina League.

In 2006 I decided to retire from playing professional baseball in order to pursue a coaching career. I was offered my first coaching position by coach Dan McDonnell, who had been an assistant coach on staff during my time at the University of Mississippi.

I have spoken at camps, clinics, and conventions all over the country. I was also honored as a guest speaker at the 2011 American Baseball Coaches Association (ABCA) national convention in Nashville, TN, where I spoke on the topic "Preparing Catchers for Success." I have also developed the Catcher's Thumb product and the Catcher's Performance Summary application for the iPhone, iPad, and iPod Touch.

With the right information and a strong work ethic, you can become a better catcher and help your team win games. The knowledge without the work ethic will not make you a better

CATCHING-101

baseball player. I encourage you to diligently practice and apply the ideas and skills covered in this book. Combining this new knowledge with hard work, you will reach your full potential as a catcher. By reading this book you will give yourself an edge on the competition and the knowledge that you need to succeed. It is your job to apply the principles covered in this book into a disciplined practice routine.

Chapter 2

Equipment

When it comes to equipment, players have a lot of choices, and it can sometimes be overwhelming trying to choose the best equipment. It's important to remember that there is no one particular *right* brand or style of equipment. You should choose your equipment based on what you like and what is comfortable to you, not what you see guys wearing on TV.

Catchers' equipment should fit correctly and be comfortable to wear. There are a lot of youth catchers wearing the wrong size equipment, and it puts them at a higher risk of injury than those who have equipment that fits properly. Parents wouldn't let their sons run onto a football field with shoulder pads and helmets that don't fit, yet many youth catchers wear equipment that is way too big or too small. All catchers' equipment should fit snugly on the body, but shouldn't be so tight as to restrict movement. When equipment fits too loosely, it tends to shift around and leave areas exposed that should be covered. Imagine how much more violent a car accident would be if a seat belt was loose instead of tight fitting! The same principle holds true for catchers' gear, so be careful when selecting your equipment. Whether we're talking about a helmet, a chest protector, shin guards, or any other piece of equipment, we want it to fit snugly on the body and be comfortable.

CATCHING-101
Mitt

Arguably our most important piece of equipment, our mitt should be considered one of our tools, just like a painter's brushes. When it comes to choosing a mitt, there are many options, so choose one based on your own personal preference. Some catchers like large mitts, while others prefer smaller ones. There is no right or wrong answer here as long as you like the mitt you use. A common misconception is that a mitt with a smaller pocket will help catchers get rid of the ball more quickly when throwing to a base, and that just plain isn't true. Throwing base stealers out has a lot to do with the pitcher, the runner, our quickness, and our mechanics; it does not have to do with the mitt. It's funny, but a lot of players will blame their glove when they miss a ball, but I've never seen a player praise his glove when he makes a great play!

The best advice I would give players looking for a new mitt is to go to a sporting goods store, try on a few mitts, and maybe even play a game of catch in the store, if possible. This is the only way to determine if you like the mitt or not. Do not choose your mitt based on what your favorite player is wearing or on color, but on what feels good on your hand.

Some catchers choose to keep their index finger outside of their mitt. This will, essentially, add an extra layer of padding to your mitt, which might be beneficial when there is a hard-throwing pitcher on the mound. This doesn't come without risks, though. Leaving our index finger outside of our mitt could make us more vulnerable to an injury, particularly when blocking. If we are late turning our mitt over to cover the five hole (we will discuss this more in the Blocking chapter), our index finger could be hit by the ball. The odds of this happening aren't very great, but if it does happen, it could be a season-ending injury.

The Complete Guide for Baseball Catchers

If you comb through the Internet, you will read about people putting different substances on their mitts to help break them in or to condition the leather. I'm not going to say that these don't work, but I believe the best way to break in a mitt is the good old-fashioned way: by playing catch with it a lot! Some of the oils and lotions can cause a mitt to get heavy over time. The tried and true method of playing catch may take a little longer to break in a mitt, but it will never cause your mitt to get heavy.

One suggestion for adding to the life of your mitt is to take excellent care of it. Whenever you're done with a practice or game, don't throw your mitt in the bottom of your bag and let it lose the shape you've worked so hard to form. Always try to keep a ball or two in the pocket and place the mitt on top of your other equipment so it won't get smashed in the bottom of your bag. Also, when you're playing catch before a practice or game and you have to set your mitt on the ground, place it with the pocket facing down so that it will stand up. Paying attention to minor details like this may help extend the life of your mitt over the course of a few seasons.

Another good idea is to have a rain mitt for days when the weather doesn't want to cooperate. I recommend that everyone who has the resources always have a backup mitt that can be used when it is rainy or muddy, or when their primary mitt has a broken lace. There is no reason to use your brand-new mitt when it is muddy outside if you don't have to.

Face Mask/Helmet

There are two different styles of headgear to choose from: the traditional two-piece mask, consisting of a skull cap and face mask, and the one-piece mask, or hockey-style mask. You will have to check your league's rules to determine if the traditional two-piece mask is allowed in your league because many leagues require a one-piece mask at the time of this writing.

CATCHING-101

Like all your equipment, your helmet should be chosen because it does a good job of protecting you and is comfortable, not because of cosmetics. The helmet should fit the player snugly and not move around when the player moves his head.

There are a few main things to look for when choosing a helmet:

Visibility: You will want to choose a helmet that allows you to clearly see the pitcher, the ball, and the playing field. Some masks have more bars, which may provide durability but offer less vision. Make sure you can see clearly out of the mask you choose.

Durability: You will want your helmet to withstand foul tips as well as more dangerous plays like getting hit by a batter's backswing or a collision at home plate. Think about these potential plays when choosing your helmet.

Weight: Wearing a heavier mask will be less comfortable than a wearing a lighter one, but it may be more durable. I have the same recommendation for helmets as I do for mitts: go into a sporting goods store and try a few on before buying one.

A common complaint about the traditional two-piece mask is that the face mask keeps slipping off the skull cap. A tip to help you prevent this situation is to put pine tar on the back of your helmet to make it sticky. It will help keep the face mask from slipping off and will also make it easier to put it on with one hand.

Chest Protector

Of all our equipment, chest protectors are probably the one piece most often worn incorrectly, especially by younger players! Chest protectors should fit snugly so they keep you protected, but if they're worn too tightly, it might cause a blocked ball to ricochet farther away. We have to find a happy medium so that the chest protector stays where we want it without being too tight.

A lot of younger players wear their chest protector so loose that it sags too low and doesn't cover their collarbone. It is important that we keep our collarbones covered so that a foul tip or a blocked ball won't hit them. It is more important to cover them than our belly. If a ball were to hit us in the belly, it probably wouldn't feel great, but we also probably wouldn't suffer an injury other than a bruise. If a ball were to hit us in the collarbone, however, we could have a broken bone, which would require us to seek medical attention and most likely miss a significant number of games. If you're having a hard time getting your chest protector to stay where you want it, try using athletic tape to keep the straps from accidentally moving.

We want to have our chest protector fit tightly enough so that it doesn't move around, but we would like to have a slight air pocket between our chest protector and our body. This air pocket will absorb some of the shock from a blocked ball and will keep the ball closer to us, which in turn will help prevent runners from attempting to advance on a blocked ball.

Some chest protectors offer firm padding, while others are much softer. This is a personal preference, just like all of our equipment choices are. Players who wear the softer chest protectors argue that the softer padding absorbs the shock of a blocked ball and prevents it from bouncing farther away, while advocates of firmer padding believe that it offers more protection. It's hard to argue with either of these opinions. You will have to decide for yourself what is more important to you: firmer padding for more protection or softer padding to keep blocked balls closer to your body.

CATCHING-101

Supportive Cup

A supportive cup is not an optional piece of equipment for catchers. One should be worn at every practice and game. Catchers are at a higher risk of injury than any other player, and this is not a piece of equipment you want to forget. Plain and simple--do not EVER catch without one!

Shin Guards

Shin guards offer leg protection from foul tips, runners sliding into home, and even the repeated motion of blocking balls in the dirt or the delivery of throwing the ball back to the pitcher from our knees. An uncomfortable set of shin guards that fit incorrectly can cause unnecessary bruises on our knees.

When choosing which shin guards to wear, make sure they are the correct length. They are not one size fits all but come in many different styles and sizes. Make sure that your knee fits snugly into the knee cup at the top of the shin guards and the bottom side flaps cover your ankles. Most adult shin guards offer two or three additional sections that cover the thigh just above the knee. They will provide additional protection from balls when we are on our knees in the blocking position.

Some youth shin guards have Velcro straps on them, but most are secured by a hook and loop. When putting on the shin guards, be sure to have the hooks on the outside of your legs. You should have a designated left and right shin guard, and they should always be worn on the same legs. This is to prevent the hooks from coming undone and hooking on each other, causing us to trip. If we fall down when we are running to back up first base, we will probably get a good laugh out of the dugout, but we will also be incapable of retrieving an overthrown ball.

The Complete Guide for Baseball Catchers

Many catchers will cross the straps on the back of their shin guards. This doesn't provide any real advantage to strapping them straight across. It is simply personal preference. If, however, you think it looks cool to have the straps crossed, go for it!

I always suggest wearing baseball pants when you are catching because the straps on the shin guards can irritate or scratch the back of your knees if you're wearing shorts. If you are catching with shorts, though, you can help prevent some irritation by hooking a few of the straps (if there are multiple straps behind the knee) in front of the shin guards instead of behind them. This will be much more comfortable, but I only recommend doing it if you're catching in shorts in a practice setting. In a game, you should always wear them the way the manufacturer designed them to be worn.

Catcher's Thumb

If you or your catcher have ever complained about a sore thumb, the Catcher's Thumb is for you. Catchers will often hyperextend their thumb in their glove for a number of reasons. One could be that the catcher was expecting the pitcher to throw a four-seam fastball, but he threw a two-seam fastball that ran or sank right into the catcher's thumb. Another might be a foul tip. Sometimes foul tips might be deflected into a catcher's thumb rather than into the pocket of the mitt. Catching the ball incorrectly is another common cause of a hyperextended or broken thumb. If you have ever suffered this, you know that it is a painful, long-lasting injury that can stay with you for an entire season.

The Catcher's Thumb is a piece of casting material that is custom molded to fit a catcher's thumb and goes inside the mitt. The idea is the same as a football mouthpiece. It comes in a standard size, but once it is dipped in warm water, it becomes flexible and can be custom molded to fit the player. It is great for rehabbing injuries, but it is also great for preventing injuries. A lot of Major League catchers wear protective thumb guards all the time so they don't have to miss games because of a possible broken thumb. Next time you're watching a Major League game, try to sneak a peek inside the catcher's mitt.

For more information about the Catcher's Thumb, please visit www.CatchersThumb.com.

Knee Savers

People often criticize knee savers because some people think they make catchers lazy. Simply put, no piece of equipment has ever made a player lazy. If the player is lazy, he was lazy before he put the Knee Savers on the back of his shin guards! I believe that Knee Savers can take stress off the knees if worn correctly. If they're worn incorrectly, they can limit mobility and prevent catchers from getting low enough in their stances.

I wore Knee Savers for a few seasons after I tore my Anterior Cruciate Ligament (ACL) in high school. I think they were excellent for taking unwanted strain off of my knees, and I recommend them to any player who has had issues with his knees.

If you're going to wear Knee Savers, you should wear them on the bottom two straps of your shin guards so they don't wedge into your knees, preventing you from squatting low to the ground. When they're worn higher on the calves, they can hinder a player's flexibility and prevent a catcher from getting as low as possible. So if you choose to wear them, just make sure that they're on the bottom two straps!

Wristbands/Sweatbands

A lot of players wear wristbands, or sweatbands, because they think they look cool. I'm not going to argue or dispute that idea, but I do think they can serve a purpose. Catchers probably sweat more than other players due to the fact that they are wearing an extra 10 pounds of equipment. This can be a problem if our hands are sweaty and we lose our grip on the ball. One way to prevent this problem is to wear a wristband so that sweat doesn't drip onto your hand, or if it does you can wipe it off.

There are even some wristbands now that have a protective shield in them, and they do an excellent job protecting your wrists while you are blocking balls. If you have had problems with your wrists or forearms, this may be an option you should consider.

Chapter 3

Stances

Catchers have three unique stances that are used over the course of a game. They are the Signal Stance, the Primary Stance, and the Secondary Stance. In all sports, it's important that athletes have proper stances that will put them into a position where they can be successful. Everyone's stances may be slightly different, but there are certain things to look for when evaluating a stance. There are many different styles of batting stances, and the same is true of catching stances. Not every catching stance has to be exactly the same, but we want to put ourselves into a strong, athletic position no matter which stance we are in.

Signal Stance

The first of our three stances is our Signal Stance. This is the stance we are in when we are relaying the signal to the pitcher. As with all our stances, we must be very comfortable in the signal stance. Over the course of a game and a season, we will be spending a lot of time in this stance, and we can't compromise our effectiveness by being uncomfortable.

Generally, when we are giving the signal to the pitcher, we want to be set up down the middle of the plate. The only time we would want to set up on either side of the plate is if we feel that the opposing team is trying to tip the pitch location. For example, if every time we shift to our left, the opposing team yells a verbal from the dugout to the hitter signaling an inside pitch (to a right-handed hitter), we may choose to give our signal on the inside corner and shift to our right or not shift at all so that the opposing team cannot see where we are set up on the plate.

Signal Stance, from front.

When we line up behind home plate, we generally want to start with our heels about six inches apart and our toes pointing toward the shortstop and second baseman. This will give us a good base and will help us properly line up our knees to the middle infielders. We do this because we only want three people on the field to see our signals: the pitcher, the shortstop, and the second baseman. Infielders may choose to shift when particular pitches are being thrown, so it is important that they always know the signal. For example, let's say we have a power-hitting right-handed hitter (RHH) at bat and a changeup is being thrown. The shortstop may want to shift to his right (into the six hole) because we are assuming that the hitter will be early on the pitch and will hopefully pull it on the ground. By moving, the infielders will be in a better position to field it. Also, we do not want runners on first base to be able to see our signs because they

CATCHING-101

might choose to steal when they know the pitcher is throwing a breaking ball or an off-speed pitch.

Now that our feet are in good position, we squat down. We are balanced on the balls of our feet, and our heels are in the air so that our thighs are parallel to the ground. We should be tall with our chest and not slouch over in order to let in as much light as possible, particularly during night games. When we play on a field with poor lighting, it is important that we give our pitcher every opportunity to see the signal we are giving him. It is frustrating for the pitcher and the catcher when signals can't be relayed properly. More important than that, however, is the fact that we do not want the pitcher to lose his tempo because he can't see our signs. When a pitcher is throwing well, we do not want to create a hiccup in his rhythm due to something that can easily be avoided.

Signal Stance, from side.

Our glove-hand forearm should be resting on the top or outside of our left thigh so that the glove becomes an extension of our leg, blocking the third base coach from looking in and seeing our signals. One common mistake that catchers make, however, is that they try to protect the signal too much and actually cause

The Complete Guide for Baseball Catchers

more harm than good by blocking the signal from the pitcher or shortstop.

We want to rest our right, or throwing-hand, forearm in the crease between our thigh and our torso. This will generally put our hand in a good position to give our signal. A good thing to do with our signal hand is to press it against our cup so we aren't giving the signal too high or too low. If the signal is given too high, base runners or coaches could easily see the sign. If it's given too low, the on-deck hitter could see the signal and relay it to the hitter.

Once we successfully relay the sign to the pitcher, we now shift into our primary or secondary stance, depending on the situation.

An important thing to remember is that we want to be consistent in how we shift into our receiving stances. Some catchers develop bad habits of shifting their bodies differently for different pitches or locations. This can cause us to relay our signs to the opposing team. For example, we might step with our left foot first whenever we throw a pitch inside to a RHH, and every time we catch a pitch away from an RHH, we might step with our right foot first. Also, some catchers have a tendency to shift differently for breaking balls as opposed to fastballs. In such cases, maybe a catcher keeps his left foot planted and steps only with his right foot for every off-speed pitch.

The easy solution for this problem is to simply do the same thing every time. If it is comfortable for you to step with your right foot and then your left foot, do it for every pitch, no matter the location or pitch called. It really doesn't matter what the sequence is as long as it is comfortable to us.

CATCHING-101

Primary Stance

The first of our two receiving stances is called the Primary Stance. We are in our primary stance when there are no runners on base and less than two strikes on the hitter.

Primary Stance, from front.

One of the most important things about all our stances is that we are comfortable in them. It is going to be hard to receive well if we are uncomfortable or feel awkward in our stance.

When we shift into our primary stance, our feet will widen and our bodies will be square to the pitcher. We generally get as low as we comfortably can while still being athletic. Keep in mind, though, that receiving stances are similar to batting stances—everybody's stance is going to be a little different, but there are certain things that must be in order for us to have success. When we set up, we want to give the pitcher the target at the batter's knees. A higher stance makes this more difficult, and we certainly don't want to give the pitcher a target in the middle of the strike zone.

The Complete Guide for Baseball Catchers

We must make sure to keep our throwing hand protected. We do this by making a fist (with our thumb inside our fingers) and placing it behind us. If it feels strange to have it behind your back, try another place like behind your ankle or knee. Our hand should never actually rest on our leg or our knee. If our hand is in open view, it can be hit by a foul ball and seriously injured.

Primary Stance, from side.

Our glove should be open to the pitcher so he has a good target to look at. We want our bodies to act as a dartboard and our mitt as the bull's-eye. Our index finger on our glove hand should be pointed at a two o'clock position. This seems to be the most natural, therefore the most effective, position. If our index finger is closer to a twelve o'clock or three o'clock position, we can get handcuffed, and it is harder to receive pitches that aren't thrown exactly where we are set up.

Secondary Stance

The second of our two receiving stances is our Secondary Stance. This is when we have runners on base, or two strikes on the hitter, and we need to be more athletic. We need to be more

CATCHING-101

athletic for two reasons: we must be able to block balls that are thrown in the dirt, and we must be able to throw runners out who attempt to steal.

In our secondary stance, we generally have our butt a little higher in the air, and our feet are a little wider apart. This makes us more athletic and better able to block and throw easily. Our feet should be not only wider but staggered. Our right foot should be positioned a little deeper than our left foot, making it easier for us to throw to a base. Generally, we shouldn't stagger our feet more than a few inches. A good guideline is that you should be able to line up the ball of your right foot with the instep of your left foot. If we "cheat" anymore than this, it can cause us to not square up to the pitcher; we will give him a bad target and it might hinder us from blocking balls to either side. Our thighs should be close to parallel with the ground, but we don't want to be so high that we give our pitcher a high target in the middle of the hitter's strike zone.

Secondary Stance, from front.

Some people choose to put their throwing hand behind their body, while some choose to put it behind their mitt. As I mentioned earlier, everyone's stance is going to be a little different, and I don't think that either is right or wrong as long as you are comfortable. We just want to make sure that our hand is protected and not in the way of getting hit by a foul ball. If one way were clearly better than the other, wouldn't all the Big League catchers on TV be doing it the same way?

Secondary Stance, from side.

Another important note on our secondary stance is that we should always position ourselves where we can see the base runners, especially when there is a left-handed batter (LHH) batting. We want to be able to see the runner on first and know if and when he is stealing. We should never fail to throw a runner out because we were unaware that he was stealing second base. It is unacceptable to not throw someone out because we relied on the first baseman or our teammates in the dugout to let us know that the runner was going. It's fine if you want to hear a verbal such as "There he goes!" or "Runner!" but that shouldn't be the only way you know he is stealing. Position yourself where you can see the runner. It is your responsibility to throw him out, not the first baseman or dugout player's responsibility–only yours!

Chapter 4

Receiving

Receiving the baseball is our most important job as catchers. You won't get a lot of credit for this from untrained spectators but it is the most valuable thing we do. It's easy for fans to notice us when we tag a runner out at the plate or throw out the fastest runner on the other team as he steals second, but neither of these things is as important as being a quality receiver. Think about it like this: how many times in a game are you going to receive a pitch? Some balls will be fouled off, some will be hit in fair territory, and some will be thrown in the dirt, but the majority of pitches that a pitcher throws are going to be caught by us. Now how many times are we going to throw a runner out at second base during a game? How many balls are we going to block during a game? We will receive pitches much more often than anything else we do throughout the game, so it's important that we do this well.

There are two important things to be conscious of when we are receiving: we want to have a quiet body and strong hands.

Quiet Body

The term "quiet" means that we want to have as little extra movement as possible. Generally, the less movement we have with our bodies, the more strikes we will get for our pitchers. Think about it from the perspective of the umpire, who is only a few inches behind us. When the pitcher throws the ball right where we are set up, we don't move very much. Even if he misses the target slightly, we shouldn't have to move. Now the pitcher misses across the plate (maybe we were set up inside, and he throws it outside). If our body remains still, or quiet, we have a better chance to get the pitch called for a strike than if we sway our body 17 inches, which is the width of the plate. We are creating the illusion that our pitcher was closer to the target if our body is quiet. If we sway a foot or more, the umpire, who is only inches behind us, sees us move and thinks to himself, "If that pitch was a strike, why did the catcher have to move so much?"

Strong Hands

The term "strong hands" means that we control the baseball, and the baseball doesn't control our mitt. In other words, we want to *stick* the pitch. "Sticking it" is when our mitt doesn't move after the ball touches it. The most important thing to remember about this is that we want to beat the ball to the spot with our mitt, as opposed to meeting the ball. When we meet the ball, our mitt has momentum and continues to move after we receive the pitch, which looks sloppy and causes us to reduce the number of strikes for our pitchers. When we beat the ball to the spot, our mitt doesn't move, and we control the pitch.

We generally want to receive with a slight bend in our elbow. When our joints are not fully extended, we are quicker. This is also the reason we start running from a crouched position, as opposed to starting with our knees locked. If we keep our elbow relaxed and not straightened or resting on our knee, we will be quicker to pitches and have more success controlling pitches by beating them to the spot. In addition to our elbow, it is a good idea to keep our glove hand relaxed, as well. Some choose to do this by making a "half-moon" with their mitt. A "half-moon" is

CATCHING-101

when we relax our glove hand and wrist before the pitcher releases the ball and our mitt slightly drops. This motion makes our mitt look like a half-moon, hence the name.

There are two situations when we may not want to receive with a slight bend in our elbow, and they have to do with the height of the pitch. We want to receive higher pitches deeper, or closer to our bodies, and we want to receive lower pitches farther away from our bodies. The reason for this is that we want to create an optical illusion of catching the ball in the strike zone. Because the pitcher's release point is higher than our mitt and because of gravity, the ball is always coming down. Therefore, the closer we catch the ball to the pitcher, the higher off the ground it will be; the deeper we catch the ball, the lower it will be. Even though we are not altering where the ball crosses the strike zone, we make these pitches look more like strikes because we are catching low pitches higher, and we are catching high pitches lower. This is particularly effective when we are receiving high breaking balls.

Receiving low pitch in Primary Stance.

Another thing we should do is to catch every pitch like it is a called third strike. Often catchers will catch a called third strike much better than they will catch any other pitch, because they are

The Complete Guide for Baseball Catchers

trying to get the umpire to ring the batter up backwards (strike him out looking). There is no excuse, however, for not giving our best effort on every pitch. Don't wait until there are two strikes on the hitter to beat the ball to the spot and control it. Do this every pitch!

Receiving high pitch in Primary Stance.

It is very important to make pitches that are strikes look like strikes and to make pitches that are balls look like balls. We NEVER want to show up the umpire! Umpires are human, and they will make mistakes, but we want to have them on our side. Imagine you are catching in the high school state championship game or playing your college rival. There may be thousands of fans at the game, and more than half of them are usually going to complain about the umpire, especially if their team loses. It is our job to take care of the umpire. We don't want to cause him any extra grief by sticking pitches that we know are balls and that we don't expect to get for a strike. When we do that, we are using our body language to tell the fans that the ball was a strike. When the umpire calls it a ball, it makes about half of the fans mad, and then they start yelling at him. Umpires are human. Put yourself in their shoes. Do you really want thousands of people yelling at you because the catcher tried to show you up? I didn't think so!

CATCHING-101

The moral of the story is to catch strikes like strikes and catch balls like balls.

If we were watching a youth baseball game and the catcher dropped the ball, we would probably hear someone from the dugout or the stands shout, "Squeeze it!" Yet when the ball pops out of our mitt, it is usually because we didn't catch the ball in the sweet spot of the mitt, not because we didn't squeeze it hard enough. If we catch the ball in the palm of the mitt instead of in the pocket (in between the index finger and thumb), there is a good possibility that the ball could pop out. To prevent that from happening, we need to concentrate on catching the ball in the sweet spot of the mitt. When we catch the ball in the sweet spot, our mitt will pop loudly. A great goal is to try to make our mitts pop more often when we receive pitches. It is immediate feedback that lets us know that we are catching the ball exactly where we are supposed to, and pitchers love to hear it because it makes them feel like they are throwing hard!

Chapter 5

Blocking

One of a catcher's most important responsibilities is blocking balls thrown in the dirt. When a pitch is thrown in the dirt, we want to use our chest protector and body to keep the ball from going to the backstop. A lot of players make the mistake of trying to use their glove to catch it off the bounce, as opposed to stopping the ball with their body. Blocking balls thrown in the dirt will help prevent pass balls and wild pitches. It's easy to see the benefit of blocking balls in the dirt when there is a runner on third base, but it's important to block balls in the dirt all the time. By keeping the ball in front of us, we can prevent wild pitches, keep double plays in order, and gain respect from our pitching staff.

Every catcher who is good at blocking anticipates the baseball being thrown in the dirt. Before a pitch is thrown, we should think to ourselves, "This ball might be thrown in the dirt; be ready to block it." By reminding ourselves of this, we are being proactive instead of reactive. Every time we call an off-speed pitch, we need to anticipate the ball being thrown in the dirt. If you're not expecting the ball to be thrown in the dirt, there is a much greater possibility you will have a delayed reaction and not make a great block. So every time we call an off-speed pitch, we should expect the ball to be thrown in the dirt and then react if it is thrown in the air.

CATCHING-101

Before the ball hits us, we must get into a good blocking position so that our body is still when we make contact with the ball. If are falling forward or moving, we will see a trampoline effect at impact that causes the ball to bounce farther away. This will result in base runners having a greater chance of taking an extra base. We want to remain balanced at all times! A lot of players make the mistake of losing their balance and falling forward onto their hands after they block the ball. When catchers end up with their hands on the ground after they block the ball, they have obviously lost their balance and were probably falling forward when the ball made contact with their chest protector.

Proper blocking position, from front.

Here are a few things we look for in a good blocking position:

Chest Leaning Slightly Forward

When we're in a good blocking position, our chest is leaning slightly forward. When we are in this position, we cause balls to be redirected toward the ground. Some players take this to the extreme and crouch down too low, causing them to be much shorter. Their thought process is that they want the ball to be deflected straight down so that it doesn't get very far away. The problem is that more balls are likely to bounce over us and get to the backstop because we have much less surface area to work with. When blocking, be sure to lean your chest only slightly forward!

Mitt Covering the Five Hole

One of the most common tendencies catchers have when blocking is to raise their mitt and try to catch the ball instead of blocking it. This is a poor practice because we do not want to expose the hole between our legs (called the five hole). Sometimes the ball will hit the back corner of the plate or hit a lump on the ground, and it will either roll on the ground or take a very small bounce. One of the cardinal sins of baseball is to let a ball go between your legs if you're a fielder, and this holds true for catchers, too.

Elbows Tucked into Sides

Another common mistake catchers make is having their arms fully extended (elbows locked out) when they're in their blocking position. When our arms are fully extended, we are usually too high because either our chest is too upright or our knees aren't spread wide enough; our mitt wouldn't reach the ground if our elbows weren't tucked into our sides. When our elbows are locked out, our arms basically form a "V" shape in front of our body. When that "V" is present, balls are much more likely to hit us in the arms. Getting it in the wrists and forearms isn't much fun and will give you unnecessary bumps and bruises. Also, when balls hit you in the wrists or forearms, they tend to deflect farther away, allowing base runners to advance.

With our elbows tucked into our sides, we expose more of our chest protector and make ourselves wider at the same time. When we add two to three inches to each side of our body, we

CATCHING-101

make ourselves wider and can stop more baseballs. Our goal is for the ball to bounce and hit us in the middle of the chest, but sometimes bounces can be erratic, so adding four to six inches of width to our bodies can be a huge benefit.

Shoulders Rounded Forward

We want our shoulders to be rounded forward (concave), as opposed to being flat or rounded backward (convex). By rounding our shoulders forward, we are trying to control where the ball bounces off us. Our goal should always be to block the ball toward home plate, and rounding our shoulders forward will help give the ball the direction we want. If our shoulders are flat or rounded backward, a ball hitting them might be deflected off to the side or toward the backstop.

Proper blocking position, from side.

Chin Tucked in

Last, we want our chin to be tucked in to the top of our chest. If we do not do this, our neck will be exposed and prone to getting hit. Getting hit in the neck can be very painful, but it is also easily prevented. Every time you block, whether in practice or in a game, be sure to tuck your chin so you won't get hit in the neck.

Now that we've discussed what a good blocking position looks like, let's cover how to get into a good blocking position. There are really two methods we can use to get into our blocking position for balls straight ahead: Falling Forward or Replacing our Feet/Knees. Each method has pros and cons, so you will have to choose which one works best for you. If you watch catchers in the Big Leagues, you will see that there is no one correct way to get into a good blocking position, and both methods are used.

Falling Forward

When our feet remain stationary and our knees drop to the ground, we call this Falling Forward. Our body weight will shift forward, and we will fall into a good blocking position, with our feet remaining in the same place. This will cause our bodies to shift forward, and we will essentially gain ground toward the ball. An advantage of falling forward is that we will shorten the distance between our body and the ball. This can possibly cut the ball off before it takes a bad bounce, particularly when it is a breaking ball. However, when fastballs are thrown, it gives us less time to get to our blocking position because we are shortening the distance between our body and the ball.

Replacing Feet/Knees

Replacing our Feet/Knees is sometimes referred to as a "kickback" because we kick our feet backward and our knees fall straight to the ground where our feet were. With this method, we do not gain ground toward the ball like we do in Falling Forward, but we give ourselves more time to get into a good blocking position and have our bodies still before impact. However, since

CATCHING-101

we are farther away, we are giving the ball more time and distance to take a bad hop and potentially get away from us.

One common misconception is that we should only block balls thrown in the dirt when there are runners on base. Actually, we should always block balls thrown in the dirt regardless of whether or not there are base runners. It's easy to see that we should try to keep runners from advancing by blocking balls when there are runners on base, but there are a number of reasons to block balls even when there are no runners on.

First, it gives our pitcher confidence that he can throw the ball in the dirt and we will block it. If we do not attempt to block balls that the pitcher throws in the dirt when no one is on base, he may think we aren't capable of blocking that ball. So when the pitcher wants to intentionally throw a ball in the dirt (maybe to get a batter to chase a pitch), he may be unsure if we can block it, and therefore he doesn't make his best pitch.

Second, it is hard to flip a switch and only block balls when runners are on base. Maybe the pitcher doesn't allow a base runner for the first three innings, and instead of blocking those balls, we try to pick them or let them go. Now it's the fourth inning and a runner reaches base. It is hard to turn the blocking "on," because we have created a habit of not blocking.

Third, there is one other guy on the field who will appreciate you blocking balls all the time, maybe even more than the pitcher–and he's standing right behind you! We want to take care of the umpire and keep balls away from him. Even though he is wearing gear, he is not expecting to be hit by balls that bounce in the dirt. If we do a good job keeping the ball in front of us, the home plate umpire will appreciate it, and it is always a good thing to have him on our side!

Last, if the first three reasons don't convince you, this one should. It is more impressive to coaches and scouts when a catcher blocks everything, whether there is a runner on third base or no runners at all. People who are watching or recruiting catchers always like guys who hustle and take charge on the field. Simply put, BLOCK EVERYTHING!

Blocking to our arm side.

When we are blocking balls thrown in the dirt to either side of home plate, our blocking posture won't change, but our mechanics will change slightly. There are two main points to remember when blocking balls that aren't directly behind home plate. First, we need to kick out and get to the ball. By this we mean that we need to push with our off-side leg (if we're blocking to the left, we push with our right leg and vice versa) and get far enough out so that the ball will hit us in the middle of our chest protector. We do not want to underestimate how far away the ball is going to be, so be sure to kick far enough out. Second, we want to get around the ball. By this we mean that we want to slightly angle our body toward home plate so the ball isn't deflected at an angle away from us but is deflected instead toward home plate.

CATCHING-101

Blocking to our glove side.

Chapter 6

Throwing to Bases

There isn't anything more satisfying than throwing out a base stealer or picking off a base runner. While catchers usually don't get much recognition for receiving pitches or blocking balls in the dirt, we do tend to be noticed when we make a great throw. A catcher who can shut down an opposing team's running game can make the difference between a good team and a great team!

A good throwing catcher has three qualities: arm strength, quickness, and accuracy.

Arm Strength

Some players have naturally stronger arms than others, but that doesn't mean that we can't strengthen our arm. Just like sprinters can become faster through training, baseball players can throw with more velocity by training their bodies to throw hard. I'm an advocate of working hard in the weight room to become the best athlete you can be, but there isn't a specific exercise you can do with weights to make yourself throw faster. One of the most common questions I get asked as a coach is, "What can I do to throw harder?" The answer is pretty simple. You must long toss- A LOT! Long toss is when a player practices throwing as far as he can to help build arm strength. Ultimately, the velocity we throw the baseball is determined by our hand speed, just as the distance we hit the ball is related to our bat speed. The only way to build hand speed is to throw far distances and gradually, over time, our hand speed will increase and so will our velocity.

While arm strength is important, our quickness and accuracy play more important roles in throwing base runners out. A player could have the strongest arm in his league, but he won't throw many base stealers out if it takes him a long time to get rid of the ball or if his throws are wild and don't go where they are supposed to.

Quickness

Quickness refers to how quickly a catcher can transfer the ball from his mitt to his throwing hand and throw it to the infielder. A catcher with a quick release will be able to throw a lot of base stealers out. When paired with a strong arm, this quickness can eliminate an opposing team's running game!

A catcher's quickness is partly due to natural athletic ability and largely due to mechanics (i.e., footwork). Good mechanics will eliminate any wasted movements and utilize the catcher's entire body when throwing.

Accuracy

Of the three qualities mentioned, accuracy is the most important-and the most overlooked-component of throwing. A catcher can have above average arm strength and quickness, but if he throws the ball wildly, he will almost never throw a runner out. When practicing throwing to bases, you should first emphasize accuracy and then work on quickness.

Too many people overemphasize pop times and do not put enough weight on accuracy. If we throw the ball to second base

The Complete Guide for Baseball Catchers

at 95 mph, but it sails into center field, we don't have a chance to throw the runner out. Accuracy first; quickness second!

When evaluating a catcher's throwing ability, don't judge him based on pop times alone; judge him by how many base stealers he throws out and how often the opposing team attempts to steal. When an opposing team respects a catcher's ability to throw base stealers out, they won't attempt to steal very often. That is usually a very good indicator of what other teams think about the catcher.

Pop time isn't important if our throw isn't accurate!

A good grip on the baseball is important when it comes to making accurate throws. A good grip will ensure that the ball travels through the air in a straight line and doesn't run or cut, causing our throw to miss the target. The correct grip catchers should use is a four-seam fastball grip, and this is true for all position players. A four-seam fastball, when thrown correctly, will have a true flight path and will fly straight. To throw a four-seam fastball, place your index finger and middle finger across the "C" or "horseshoe" on the baseball, keeping your thumb underneath. A two-seam fastball looks very similar to this, but the index and middle fingers go across the narrow seams on the baseball. Getting a good four-seam grip is important for accuracy!

Some players have a hard time getting a four-seam grip on the ball quickly. A good drill for this is to practice flipping the ball to

CATCHING-101

yourself and getting a correct grip over and over. Just like any other part of our game, our grip can improve with practice.

Left: correct four-seam grip; Right: incorrect four-seam grip.

Another area we need to emphasize is getting true backspin when we throw. True backspin is when the ball spins straight up and down and is caused by keeping our hand "behind the baseball" and having a good arm slot when we throw. Balls thrown with true backspin will stay straight and in the air longer and will carry farther than balls with sidespin. When a ball has sidespin, it will move in the air similar to a sinker or cutter that a pitcher might throw. When we keep our hand "behind the baseball," our fingers are directly behind the baseball at our release point, and we throw a ball with true backspin. When we are "on the side of the baseball," our fingers are slightly on the outside of the ball, causing it to spin sideways.

Every time we throw the baseball, whether loosening up before a game, throwing the ball back to the pitcher, or throwing to second base in between innings, we should ALWAYS try to get the ball to have perfect backspin.

The Complete Guide for Baseball Catchers

Throwing to First Base

Over the course of an entire season, we are probably not going to pick many runners off first base. However, that doesn't mean we shouldn't practice it or attempt to do in a game. We just need to realize that picking a runner off first base is a very low percentage play, and we need to choose wisely when to do it.

Pitchers will throw a pickoff to first base to try to prevent runners from stealing. That helps us if it slows down the opposing team's running game, but it doesn't mean we should pick off for the same reason. Catchers should only try to pick a runner off first base if we believe we have a realistic chance of throwing him out. It is such a low percentage play that we aren't going to pick many runners off, and it isn't worth making unnecessary throws just to threaten the other team. To maintain the element of surprise, it is best to selectively choose when we pick off. Catchers who throw to first base too often lose the element of surprise and will be less successful picking off.

When we pick off to first base, we can either choose to throw standing up or on our knees. If we throw standing up, we are more likely to make a stronger throw because we can use more of our leg strength. But when we throw from our knees, we are more likely to catch the runner off guard. We should be able to throw to first base both ways because different situations call for different types of throws.

Throwing standing up requires less arm strength than throwing from our knees, but it can still be very effective. Once we receive the pitch, we want to make sure that our shoulders, hips, and feet are all lined up directly at first base. As we are turning our body to throw, we want our right foot to land directly under our center of gravity. This will allow us to get rid of the ball quickly and also be able to generate velocity with our leg muscles. It is only a

CATCHING-101

fraction of a second difference, but our right foot should land first, and then our left foot should land. If we simply *hop* and both of our feet land at the same time, we will have lost our momentum and won't be able to utilize our leg strength.

Throwing to first base standing up; right foot lands under our chin.

Throwing from our knees can be slightly more difficult and is more appropriate for catchers who are a little older and have enough arm strength to still make a firm throw. There are two options when throwing from our knees: we can either drop our left knee or our right knee first. By choosing to drop our left knee first, we will have a slightly quicker release, but we could be sacrificing velocity. However, if we choose to drop our right knee first and then let our left knee follows, we will be able to make a slightly stronger throw. This is because when our right knee lands first, we can push off of it just like we would if we were standing up. Picture how we use our right foot to drive and generate energy when we are standing up and throwing. Well, there is no difference when we are on our knees. By choosing to drop our right knee first, we can use it to create momentum toward our target, first base. Catchers who have stronger arms may feel comfortable throwing with only their left knee on the ground, but if we want to make a stronger throw, we should drop our right knee first.

We should be especially prepared to pick a runner off first base after a failed sacrifice bunt attempt. When the opposing team attempts a sacrifice bunt, the base runner at first base will usually be aggressive with his lead and be farther away from first base. If the batter foul tips, or takes the pitch, we should be prepared to pick the base runner off because he is likely to have a larger than normal lead.

When there is an RHH batting, it is usually easier to pick off to first base because there is no obstacle in the way like there is with an LHH. Some catchers feel uncomfortable picking off when there is an LHH, however, base runners are aware of this and may try to take advantage by taking a larger lead or being a little more lackadaisical when an LHH is batting. This could possibly be an opportunity to pick off a runner who is not expecting us to throw because an LHH is batting.

Throwing to first base dropping our right knee first.

CATCHING-101
Throwing to Second Base

Whether we are trying to pick a runner off second base or throw a base stealer out, our mechanics when throwing the ball to second base will be the same. There are three distinct ways to throw the ball to second base, but one method stands out as having the most number of advantages. The three different sets of mechanics are: the Replacement Method, the Pivot, and the Jab Step. In each of these methods, our footwork, or our lower half, will be different, but how we transfer the ball from our mitt to our throwing hand should be the same no matter which method we use.

The Replacement Method refers to when we hop and replace our left foot with our right foot. This is a very common way to throw to second base. However, there are a few disadvantages to using this method. First, when we replace our left foot with our right foot, we are shifting our body weight toward the third base dugout instead of toward second base. Many players who use this set of mechanics will find themselves in the right-handed batter's box as they are throwing. Ideally, we would like to keep all our momentum in a straight line with home plate, the pitching mound, and second base. Another disadvantage to using the replacement method is that many players don't actually replace their left foot with their right foot, but instead their right foot actually ends up farther back (away from second base) because they are trying to be too quick. This is bad because we aren't utilizing the strongest muscles in our body, our legs!

The Pivot Method is when a player simply pivots on his right foot from his secondary stance and throws the ball to second base. Some players will do this only on pitches that are thrown on the first base side of their body, like a fastball away from an RHH or a right-handed slider that is cutting into the left-handed batter's box. An advantage of using this set of mechanics is that we can get rid of the ball more quickly because we are only taking one step, as opposed to taking two steps with the other methods.

The Complete Guide for Baseball Catchers

However, without a lot of practice, it can be very difficult to consistently repeat where our front, or left, foot lands. We want it to land directly in front of our pivot, or right, foot and in line with second base. Often, players do not work on this set of footwork in practice yet will attempt it in a game. Not practicing it enough will result in inconsistency with our left foot, and we will either land open or closed, causing us to make a poor throw.

High transfer using the Pivot Method

It's important to plant our left foot in a straight line to 2B.

CATCHING-101

The Jab Step method is when a catcher takes a small step forward with his right foot in the middle of his body in order to gain ground and momentum toward second base. When done correctly, our right foot will land directly under our chin. Any step farther than that will be counterproductive because we won't gain any additional velocity on our throw, and it will take us longer to release the ball because of the increased distance that we step. Many young players believe that taking a bigger step will let them throw the ball harder, but it doesn't outweigh the extra time taken to release the ball. By taking a jab step under our chin, we are gaining some ground to second base, and we are also controlling our momentum by not allowing it to shift to either side but going directly toward our target, second base.

When using the Jab Step we should place our right foot under our chin.

Any of these methods can yield positive results, and what is best for one player may not necessarily be best for another. However, the jab step method seems to be the easiest for players to consistently repeat, and the easiest for new catchers to learn.

We want our transfer to be as quick as possible, but we also want to have a high transfer. A low transfer is when we exchange the ball from our mitt to our throwing hand around the height of our stomach, and a high transfer is when we exchange the ball around the height of our shoulders or above. A low exchange is going to be slower than a high one and will encourage a longer arm action, which is not advantageous to us since we are trying to throw out a sprinting base runner. Once we receive the ball, we should pull our mitt toward our right ear and try to transfer the ball into our throwing hand as soon as possible. The sooner we can get the ball out of our mitt and into our throwing hand, the more time we will have to get a proper four-seam grip on the ball. When we do it correctly, we should look similar to a quarterback who receives the snap and immediately takes the football to his back shoulder, never letting the ball drop to the height of his stomach.

When we use the Jab Step method we stay directly behind home plate.

There will be situations when we are trying to throw the ball to second base and the batter has stepped over home plate. When this happens, there is no way to avoid contact with the batter, but we want to do our best to prevent an injury from occurring. If we simply try to throw over the batter, we may possibly find that our throwing hand will make contact with his bat, helmet, or body. This contact can cause the small bones in our hand and fingers to break, and we might even miss the rest of the season. If contact is

CATCHING-101

unavoidable, we should try to make body-to-body contact because there is a much smaller chance that we will get injured that way. This should only be done when contact is unavoidable; it is not a way to try to cheat the system and force the umpire to make an interference call.

Throwing to Third Base

While most players and coaches spend more practice time throwing to second base than to first or third, throwing the ball to third base is arguably the most important throw. That is because a poor throw to third when a base stealer is attempting to steal is almost always going to result in the other team scoring a run. While a poor throw to second base could allow the runner to advance to third base, there is still a possibility that we could end the inning with the runner stranded at third base and no run being scored.

Opposing teams will usually attempt to steal third base when there is an RHH at bat because he is an obstacle between third base and us. That doesn't mean we shouldn't be prepared to throw just because there is an LHH at bat. When there is an LHH batting, our throwing mechanics to third base are fairly simple. We can choose to either pivot on our right foot and throw, or we can take a slight jab step directly at third base with our right foot first, in order to gain some ground and get our momentum working in a straight line to our target.

This gets a little more complex when there is an RHH batting, though. First, we should know the rule that the batter isn't required to duck or move out of the batter's box to avoid our throw. It is our responsibility to throw around him. This is what we will base our mechanics on, having to avoid the batter and still be as efficient as possible.

The Complete Guide for Baseball Catchers

We always want to throw from foul territory, or from behind the batter, whether we are trying to throw a base stealer out or pick off a runner. A common mistake players make is to step in front of the batter and home plate in order to throw the ball to third base. There are two reasons why we don't throw from in front of home plate. First is because we would have to gain more ground and take an extra step to clear ourselves of the batter, as opposed to stepping behind him. The second reason is because base runners are always taught to take their lead off third base in foul territory so that if a line drive hits them it will be a foul ball, not an out; and then they return to the base in fair territory. If we were to step in front of home plate, we would be in fair territory, as would the runner. This wouldn't give us a clear lane for throwing the ball to our third baseman, because all three of us would be standing in a straight line. If the runner is running back to the base in fair territory and we step behind an RHH to throw the ball, we would then have a clear lane to make a throw to our third baseman.

Our right foot should land behind our left foot and our momentum should be going to third base, not the third base dugout.

Just like when we are throwing to second base, we want to step with our right foot first. If our first step is with our left foot, we

CATCHING-101

will be required to take an extra step, which will cost us valuable time when attempting to throw someone out. Our right foot will cross over behind our left foot, and our left foot will step directly to third base. One common mistake players make is to have both feet step directly toward the third base dugout instead of toward third base. As with every throw we make, our momentum should be directed toward our target.

Chapter 7

Plays at Home Plate

Tag Plays at the Plate

Tag plays at home plate are the most exciting plays in all of baseball. However, they are potentially the most dangerous play in baseball if the right mechanics are not used. Therefore, our goal during a tag play at home plate should be to remain in a protected position at all times and to get the runner out.

Of all the different mechanics presented in this book, tag plays at the plate are probably the most technically difficult. Unlike the mechanics of our primary stance or how we get to a good blocking position, the mechanics of these plays shouldn't be much different from player to player. These steps should be followed very closely to ensure that we do not get injured.

If there is ever a potential play at the plate (e.g., runner on first and batter hits a double, or runner on second and batter hits a single to outfield), we MUST keep our face mask and helmet on at all times! There should never be a situation where there is going to be a play at the plate and you get caught without your mask on.

Once the ball is hit and we believe there is going to be a play at

CATCHING-101

home plate, we should briefly remain in foul territory behind home plate. We do this because we want to watch the play develop, and our peripheral vision is wider the farther back we stand. This will allow us to view key parts of the play without having to move our head. For example, the easiest plays seem to come from left field because we can clearly see the ball, our outfielder, the third base coach, and the runner. On the other hand, catchers seem to misplay balls coming from right field more often because they take their eye off the ball to check on the runner and then try to find the ball again. An important person to watch is the third base coach. By paying attention to him, we can learn if he is going to send the runner home or hold him up at third base. If he decides to hold him up at third base, we may want to have the throw from the outfield cut off and possibly thrown to another base.

When we know there is going to be a play at the plate, we will position ourselves in a good fielding position and be ready to receive the throw. We should start with our left heel about six inches in front of the third base side point on home plate, and our body should be square to whichever fielder is throwing us the ball. So, if we are receiving a throw from left field, we would keep our chest square to left field; if the throw is coming from right field, our chest should be square to right field. We should be in an athletic position where we're balanced and ready to catch a throw that is high, low, left, or right (similar to a first baseman).

The reason we stand in front of home plate, instead of in the middle of the baseline, is because we want to give the runner a clear view of home plate. If we do not have the baseball, we do not want to obstruct the runner and give him a reason to run over us. Even though this is illegal before you get to professional baseball, almost all catchers have been run over at some point. By giving the runner a clear vision of home plate, we encourage them to touch home plate or slide into home plate without causing a collision.

The Complete Guide for Baseball Catchers

The ball will either be thrown to us in the air or on a short hop, a long hop, or an in between hop. In between hops are the most challenging plays to make because we sometimes get handcuffed and don't know whether or not to be aggressive to the ball or to field it more conservatively. If you're ever in doubt, be aggressive to the ball and try to pick it out of the dirt like a first baseman would.

Getting ready for a throw coming from right field.

Sometimes players will miss the baseball because they rush the catch in order to tag the runner out. Be sure to catch the ball first and then worry about applying the tag to the runner. A cardinal sin is to miss the baseball because we are trying to be too quick with our tag!

Once we have caught the baseball, we will then take away the runner's clear path to home plate by placing our left foot on the foul line with our toes pointed toward the runner. In order to keep ourselves protected, we must have our toes pointed directly at the base runner who is trying to score. This is often done incorrectly, and players end up exposing their ankles and the inside of their knees to the runner. We step directly toward the runner for two reasons. First, our shin guards protect the front of

CATCHING-101

our legs very well, but often leave the sides exposed and subject to injury. We want the hard molded plastic to stay between us and the runner's cleats! Second, our knees are built to bend front to back. If there is a collision at the plate and our cleats get stuck in the ground, this could be very bad if our toes aren't pointed toward the runner.

Left: getting ready for throw from CF; Right: Taking away the runners lane.

If at all possible, we want to tag the runner with two hands. There could be a situation where you do not have time or cannot reach the runner with two hands, but it is important to do because it will prevent the ball from popping out of our mitt when we tag him. We would like to have our throwing hand on the ball and inside of our mitt to hold it securely. Sometimes players will try to squeeze their mitt shut with their throwing hand, but if we "snow-cone" the ball, it could still pop out and cause the runner to be safe.

As we go to tag the runner, some players will choose to drop their right knee on the ground, and some will remain standing on two

The Complete Guide for Baseball Catchers

feet. By staying on both feet, you will be more athletic and will be able to throw more quickly to another base, if needed. Always tag the runner firmly. We aren't trying to tag him so hard that it starts a fight, but we don't want the umpire to question if we really tagged him or not. By placing a firm tag on the runner, we let everyone in the ballpark know that we tagged him.

Dropping our right knee for tag play at home.

If the play at home plate is the third out of the inning, you should show the ball to the umpire and wait for him to call the runner out before jogging off the field. However, if there are less than two outs, you should look to see if there is another possible play. An example is throwing the batter runner out at second base.

The ball is not always thrown on line to home plate; sometimes it is thrown up the third base line, and other times it is thrown up the first base line. This is how we handle each of those situations:

You need to catch balls thrown up the third base line when you are in fair territory, as opposed to backing up to catch them in foul territory. You may think that the bounce will be easier to field the farther back you are but then you run the risk of letting the ball and the base runner collide. If the ball were to hit the

CATCHING-101

base runner and ricochet far away, we would have to retrieve it because it is live and the ball is still in play. The base runner will almost always score in this instance. Also, the runner is generally running in foul territory because they took a turn around third base (unless they're scoring on a sacrifice fly). If we are in between the runner and home plate and we do not have the ball, there is a good chance that there could be a collision. We want to avoid that at all costs.

When we are dealing with balls that are thrown up the first base line, we need to keep our left foot as close to the front (3B side of home plate) as possible, even if it forces us to make a backhand play. Catchers often field this ball incorrectly by leaving home plate and fielding the ball in the middle of their body. When we leave our position at home plate, it creates a larger distance between the base runner sliding into home and us. A lot of times, this is the difference between tagging the runner out and watching him slide in safely. Once we catch the backhand ball, we can turn and make a tag, as opposed to being five or six feet away or farther and possibly having to dive to make the play. Catching a backhand ball can be more difficult than catching a forehand, so be sure to practice catching these balls in practice!

Proper mechanics to field ball thrown up the first base line.

The Complete Guide for Baseball Catchers

A throw coming from an outfielder could easily be 200 to 250 feet long. When throws are that long, they have plenty of time to run or cut while they're in the air. Balls thrown from outfielders will generally run to the fielder's arm side while in the air. It's important to know this because we want to read the ball as early as we can to see if it is going to be off line or on target. Left-handed outfielders' balls will usually run toward the first base side of the field, and right-handed throwing outfielders' balls will generally run toward the third base side of the field. If there isn't going to be a play at home plate because the throw is off line, we should tell the cut-off man (one of our infielders) to cut the ball off and possibly throw it to another base.

If the throw is going to get to us late or the runner gets held up at third base and there is not going to be a play at home plate, we should either have the ball cut off by an infielder or do anything we can to keep the ball in front of us. This is the only time we would want to drop to our knees and block the ball with our body. If there is ever a potential play, we want to try to use our glove to catch the ball so that we have a real chance of tagging the runner out.

Each team may have different verbals for when the catcher wants the ball to go through or to be cut off, so make sure that you and all of your infielders know what each verbal means. The most common verbal a catcher uses when he wants the ball cut off is "Cut! Cut!" If you want the ball to be thrown to another base, the number of that base would usually follow the command. For example, if you want the ball cut off by the infielder and thrown to second base you might shout, "Cut 2, Cut 2!" The verbal "Relay!" is generally used when you want your cut off man to catch it and then throw the ball to home plate. We might do this if the throw is slightly off line, but we still have a chance to throw the runner out because he will not beat the throw to home plate. If the outfielder makes a good throw and we don't want our cut-off man to do anything, we simply wouldn't say anything and that would let the infielder know not to touch the ball. Some teams will use the verbal "let it go" when they don't want the ball to be cut off. Which particular set of verbals we use isn't nearly as important as making sure that our entire team knows what they mean so that we can properly communicate with each other.

Force Plays at Home Plate

There are two main techniques we use when we have a force play at home plate. We will assume that there are less than two outs for this play, because if there are already two outs, the fielder should make the easiest play and that usually isn't at home plate. We will break this down into two categories: balls to the corners of the infield (1st and 3rd) and balls to the middle of the field (Pitcher, SS, and 2B).

Force play at home plate coming from the third baseman.

On balls that are hit to the corners of the infield, we act like a first baseman. We receive the ball in fair territory with our right foot on the base, just as a right-handed first baseman would receive a ball thrown to him. One thing to remember is that we generally start with both feet on home plate and then, when the ball is

The Complete Guide for Baseball Catchers

thrown, we step toward it to gain ground. It is important that we don't extend too early but wait and see where the ball is thrown. If we extend too early and a ball isn't thrown directly on line with us, we will have a hard time handling it, and we won't have as good a chance to make the play.

The play is a little different for us on balls hit to the middle of the field. On these balls, we have an opportunity to turn the double play, so we want to put ourselves in a good position for throwing to first. We do this by starting behind home plate, then coming across and sweeping our right foot over the plate when we receive the ball or slightly after. Just as we did with throws from the corners, we do not want to extend too early and run the risk of mishandling a bad throw. Once we see that the throw is on line with us, we step into fair territory and sweep our foot across home plate. By doing this, we create a throwing lane to first base, just as we would do with a bunt down the first base line.

Force play at home plate when the throw is coming from P, SS, or 2B.

In the event of a bad throw, it is our job to get the out at the plate and not worry about turning the double play. When a ball is hit to the middle of the field and the fielder makes a poor throw to us, we again become like a first baseman and make sure that we

CATCHING-101

receive the ball with our foot on home plate. It is unacceptable to not get an out because we were trying to turn the double play.

When we are certain we have no chance of turning the double play, we should make a full arm fake to first and then look to third, and not just concede the play. Often the runner at third will make too big a turn when he sees our arm action to first, and we will have a chance to throw him out at third base. If we arm fake to first, then look to third and there is no play there, nothing is lost. The runner at first was already going to be safe, and we just tried to fool the runner at third into taking an extra big turn around the base. It is important that you are always ready to throw the ball to third. You cannot be unprepared or timid about throwing to third when the runner does exactly what we want him to do-get so far off third base that we can't throw him out.

Getting Run Over

At almost all levels of baseball, it is illegal for a base runner to cause a malicious collision at home plate. However, it happens all the time, and if our mechanics are poor, we leave ourselves at risk of a major injury. Catchers get hurt when they try to act tough during this play and deliver a blow to the base runner. The base runner has a running start and we are standing still. We must understand that fact in order to get run over without getting hurt. This is not the time to show everyone how tough we are!

When a base runner is coming home and he is going to try to take us out, we MUST be in a crouched position that makes us lower than he is. If our center of gravity is higher than the base runners, we open ourselves up to serious injury. At impact we should try to shift our weight from the balls of our feet to our heels, rolling backwards. This will help change the direction of the shock, as opposed to holding our ground and absorbing all of it.

The Complete Guide for Baseball Catchers

If you know there is going to be a collision at the plate, catch the ball first and then get into a safe position and apply the tag.

Proper position when preparing for a collision at home plate.

Chapter 8

Pop Flies

There are many important things to remember about catching pop flies. The first thing we'll talk about is anticipating where the ball is going to be. Generally, if there is an RHH, a pop fly to the catcher is going to be on the first base side of the field, and if there is an LHH, the pop fly is going to be on the third base side. Knowing this can help us find the ball in the air more quickly. If an RHH fouls a ball off, we should look first to the first base side of the field. While we are looking for the ball, we should take our mask off and hold it in our throwing hand. This will allow us to have a clearer view.

One of the most important things to remember about catcher pop flies is that we should turn our back toward the infield so that we are actually facing the backstop when we are catching the ball. We do this because of the ball's spin. Balls that are hit straight up have extreme backspin, which will cause the ball to "come back" to the infield. So, in theory, a ball hit straight up over the plate will reach its highest point, and on the way down it will move toward the pitcher's mound. If we try to catch the ball while facing the infield, the ball will be moving away from us. So we remedy that by facing the backstop or turning our back to the infield. Now, because of the extreme backspin the ball has, the ball will come back toward us, and it is much easier to catch a ball that is coming toward us than it is to catch a ball that is falling away from us.

Proper position to catch a pop fly.

Now that we have located the ball and put ourselves in a good position to field it, we should anticipate where it is going to land and keep in mind that the ball is going to come back to the infield. When the ball gets to its highest point, we should call for it, using the terminology our team uses to call for pop flies (e.g., "I got it!" "Ball!" or "Mine!"). This is when we throw our mask away from where the ball is going to land. We do not want to drop it beside us because we do not want to step on it and risk an injury. Throw it away from where the play is going to happen so that there is no way you could step on it.

When we are actually catching the ball, there are two main things we should remember. One, we must keep our feet moving. Should the wind carry the ball away from where we originally think it is going to land or we miscalculate where it is going to land, we want to be able to move quickly to make the catch. If we try to catch the ball with our feet stationary, it is much harder to move than it is if we keep our feet moving. With our feet moving, we can quickly move to position ourselves under the ball. The

CATCHING-101

next thing to remember is that we want to catch the ball like an outfielder, above our head and with two hands. We do this for the same reason that outfielders do this. It is harder to misplay the ball with our hands over our head, and we can watch the ball all the way into the glove. Also, we can use our mitt to block the sun if the flight of the ball crosses through the sun.

For pop flies that are close to the backstop, dugout, or fence, we should use our throwing hand to "find the fence." We do this by placing our hand out and using it to determine if we are close to the fence or not. Another important thing to remember about a ball in this area is that we should sprint to where we think it is going to land and not try to time it. Great catches are made by being in position early and reaching over dugout rails or fences if necessary, not by trying to time the play and diving into dugouts or over fences.

Balls should always be assumed to be catchable. It is unacceptable to let a ball drop in the playing field because you thought it was going to go out of play.

Catchers have other responsibilities on pop flies hit in foul territory, as well. We should let our teammates know if a ball is going to be in play or outside the fence. We have the best view of the field so it is important that we help them out and let them know how much room they have before they get to the fence. We can put ourselves in a better position to see the ball if we run toward the fence that the ball could possibly cross. For example, if the ball is hit in foul territory and the right fielder is running to catch the ball, we should run toward the first base dugout and let the outfielder know if he is approaching the fence. You can use whatever verbal your team uses (e.g., "Fence!" or "You've got room!"). There is one very important thing we must remember, though. If there is a runner on third base with less than two outs, we must stay at home so that the runner cannot tag and go home on a caught ball. If there are two outs, we should try to help our other fielder, though. If the ball is caught, it's the third out of the inning and the inning is over; if the ball is not caught, it's a foul ball and the runner cannot tag and run home.

In the event of a long foul ball that our outfielders run after, be sure to give them plenty of time to return to their position before letting the pitcher throw the next pitch. One reason for this is that we want our outfielder in the correct position so that a batted ball doesn't land where he should be able to make a play; and two, we want to give him a few moments to catch his breath after running 80 or 100 feet. After a foul ball, we should always pay attention to our fielders and make sure they're in position before we give a signal to the pitcher.

Chapter 9

Fielding Bunts

Fielding a bunt is usually a pressure play, not because of the difficulty of the skill but because of *when* teams usually bunt. Fielding bunts can be difficult because it is much harder to bunt during a game than during practice, and bunts usually happen during a pressure situation in a game. Generally, when the score is 11-2 in the third inning, there aren't many bunts taking place, but when it is a tie or one-run ball game in the seventh, eighth, or ninth inning, teams are more likely to bunt.

There are a few things we must do when fielding any bunted ball. First, we must position our body so that we are ready to throw when we field the ball. If we plan on fielding a bunt and throwing it to first base, before we field the ball we must make sure that our feet and body are lined up and we are ready to make a throw. When we're in a good throwing position, our feet, hips, and shoulders are all pointed directly at our target (think of a pitcher throwing out of the stretch). Our body should be lined up when we field the ball so that we do not have to turn our hips and shoulders to our target; they should already be in line. The most common mistake catchers make when fielding bunts is that we field the ball with our chest square to the target and spin to get to a proper throwing position. When we do this, we will make a poor throw.

The Complete Guide for Baseball Catchers

Second, we should field the ball with two hands, using our throwing hand to rake the ball into our mitt. There may be a situation when the batter made an excellent bunt and we have to bare hand the ball or we will not have a shot at throwing him out, but in most situations, we should use two hands. Using two hands will reduce our chance of mishandling the ball. If you were asked to field 300 bunts and you could field 100 of them using only your glove, 100 of them using only your throwing hand, and 100 of them using your mitt and your throwing hand, which way would you have the most success? You would probably mishandle fewer balls using both hands!

Another time when it is usually OK to field the ball bare-handed is when it has come to a complete stop. When the ball is completely stopped and we are going to field it with our throwing hand, we want to use the Push/Pull method. This means that we should try to push the ball into the ground and then pull it up. The reason we use this technique is to ensure that we have a proper grip on the ball and that we don't bobble it. Usually when players try to field the ball bare-handed and then bobble it, they have taken their eye off the ball too early and looked up to see where the base runner was. Field the ball first, and then focus on the target you are throwing to.

Also, we should always sprint toward the ball. There is no excuse to jog after the ball, even if it only a few feet away from us. When the ball is in play and there is a runner sprinting toward first base, we must sprint after the ball to field it as quickly as possible.

Finally, in the event that we cannot field the ball, we must communicate loudly and clearly to our other fielders so they know where to throw the ball or what to do. We are the only player on the field who can see each play as it develops, so we need to let our teammates know what to do when they field the ball.

CATCHING-101
Bunts to 1B

Balls bunted down the first base line are unique because there is an added element that we need to be conscious of–the base runner himself. The Runner's Lane is three feet wide, starts halfway down the baseline, and is in foul territory. This is where the runner is supposed to run. However, most runners don't run in this lane because it makes our throw easier, so they run in fair territory, which is illegal. If the runner is running in the runner's lane and we hit him with the ball when we throw it, the ball is still live and the runner will most likely be safe at first base. However, if he is running in fair territory and our throw hits him, he is supposed to be out. We don't want to put ourselves in a position where we rely on the umpire to decide if the runner was running in the runner's lane or not.

Correct: using two hands and body is squared to our target.

Once the ball has been bunted, we should sprint directly to it and turn our body so that our shoulders, hips, and feet are all pointing directly to our target, first base. The next thing we want to do is to clear a path between ourselves and the first baseman so the runner doesn't interfere with our throw. We do this by taking

The Complete Guide for Baseball Catchers

one extra step that moves us away from the foul line and toward first base. This will clear a lane for us to make a clean throw to the first baseman.

We should remember to communicate with the pitcher and other infielders who could be attempting to field the ball. If we want to field it, we should be sure to scream the verbals used by our team (e.g., "I've got it!" or "Mine!") and also scream, "Inside, inside!" to the first baseman to let him know that he should be standing on the inside part of first base.

Bunts Back to the Pitcher

Fielding a bunt back to the pitcher with our body square to 1B.

We have the option of using one of two different sets of footwork when fielding balls that are bunted toward the middle of the field. The way we handle this is based partly on where the ball is bunted and partly on personal preference. We may choose to field balls bunted slightly to the first base side of the field like a ball bunted to first and make a clockwise turn around the ball. Balls bunted slightly toward the third base side of the field may be fielded like a ball bunted to third base, where we make a

CATCHING-101

counter-clockwise turn around the ball. Balls that are bunted directly back toward the pitcher can be fielded either way.

We should sprint directly to the ball but then slightly round it with our last step or two. A lot of players make the common mistake of taking too big a turn to get around the ball. Remember, the shortest distance between two points is a straight line, so we want to sprint on as straight a line as possible. Then, whether we make a clockwise or a counter-clockwise loop around the ball, we want to have our feet ready in a position to the throw the ball before we rake the ball into our mitt.

Bunts to 3B

Balls bunted down the third base line are most commonly mishandled or thrown away. There are two reasons for this. First, it is a longer throw to first base than it is for the other bunts. And second, players do not get into a good position to throw before they field the ball. By this we mean that players field the ball with their back toward the first baseman, forcing them to have to spin and throw at the same time without setting their feet.

Taking an extra step past the ball bunted to 3B.

To ensure that we make good throws, we will need to field this ball just like any other bunt. Before we field the ball, we need to have our body in position to throw to our target. This is a little more difficult on a ball bunted down the third base line because if we sprint straight to the ball and field it, we will not be in position to throw to first base. We must take an extra step past the ball with our right foot so that we can pivot and get our momentum going directly to first base.

We do not spin and throw; be sure to get your feet set towards 1B.

Once we field the ball, we should not just spin and throw. We must take a small shuffle toward first base. This will improve our accuracy and add velocity, and keep us from being unbalanced when we throw the ball.

Blocked Third Strikes

There is one more situation that is similar to fielding bunts and that is fielding blocked third strikes. Even though a blocked third strike isn't a bunted ball, we are going to field it the same way we would field a bunt.

CATCHING-101

When first base isn't occupied by a base runner or there are two outs and first base is occupied, the batter can run to first base on a third strike that the catcher doesn't catch in the air. This usually happens when the batter chases a breaking ball in the dirt and we have to block it. If we block the ball and it rolls into fair territory, we will field it just as we would any other bunt. However, if the ball rolls into foul territory on the first base side of the field, we will have slightly different footwork.

We need to be conscious of the batter runner when making our throw, just as we would with a ball bunted down the first base line. Since the runner's lane is in foul territory, the batter runner could possibly be between the first baseman and us. As soon as we recognize that the ball is going to roll into this area, we need to let our first baseman know that he needs to take our throw in foul territory and keep his right foot on first base. The common verbal that most teams use is "Outside, outside!" to remind the first baseman to field the ball on the outside part of the base.

Fielding a blocked third strike in foul territory.

To create a clear lane between the first baseman and us, we may need to take an extra step toward the first base dugout.

The Complete Guide for Baseball Catchers

Sometimes we may need to take more than one step, and that is perfectly fine. The most important thing we can do is create a clear lane to throw to the first baseman and be loud when reminding the first baseman to take the throw on the outside part of the base.

Chapter 10

Pass Balls/Wild Pitches

For the purpose of this book, we are going to treat pass balls and wild pitches the same. They are scored differently, but they are essentially the same thing and should be fielded the same way. Technically, a passed ball is when a runner advances due to the catcher letting a ball get past him that he should have caught. A wild pitch is when a runner advances because the pitch couldn't be handled without an extraordinary effort.

As a catcher, our goal should be to minimize the total number of pass balls and wild pitches. If we work hard to improve our receiving and blocking, we will reduce our total number of wild pitches and pass balls.

It is easy to see how our team is affected when there is a runner on third base and a ball gets to the backstop, allowing the runner to score. There are other situations, however, that aren't always obvious to the casual fan, when these missed balls really hurt our team. If there is a runner on first base and a ball gets by us, it may appear that no real damage was done. However, we have now taken away the double play situation that could have potentially changed the inning. If there are less than two outs and a runner on second base, a passed ball or wild pitch may allow the runner to get to third base and score on a sacrifice fly. The opposing team doesn't even have to get another hit to drive the run in. Maybe the opposing team was going to sacrifice bunt the base runner to the next base, but instead the runner advanced on a passed ball or wild pitch, so they're no longer going to sacrifice one of their outs.

Sometimes when a ball gets by us, it can be difficult to locate, so we want to know which verbals our team uses to let us know the location of the ball. The common verbals most teams use are "Three!" for a ball on the third base side of the field, "One!" for a ball on the first base side of the field, "Under!" or "Feet!" for a ball that is around the catcher's feet, and "Back!" for a ball that has gone straight behind them. Using verbals like "Right!" or "Left!" is discouraged because the pitcher's left side is the catcher's right side. Using those verbals can be confusing to everyone involved and could easily be the cause of miscommunication.

When the ball has gotten behind us, either because of a failed block attempt or an errant pitch, we want to locate the ball and then sprint toward it. We may also choose to take off our mask so that we don't have anything obstructing our vision. When there is a runner on third base, we should slide on our shin guards instead of running toward the ball and bending over to pick it up because this will allow us to field the ball more quickly.

As we are sliding on our shin guards, we should keep a few things in mind:

Field it Like a Bunt

When we field bunts, we are standing on our feet and not sliding on our shin guards; however, that's not what we mean by "Field it Like a Bunt." We mean that we should field the ball by raking it into our mitt with our throwing hand, the same way we field bunts. We want to rake the ball into our mitt for the same reasons

CATCHING-101

we do when fielding bunts–because we are more likely to field the ball cleanly and not mishandle it.

Proper form when fielding a Pass Ball/Wild Pitch.

Throw it Like a Dart

We must field this ball and get rid of it as quickly as possible so the runner doesn't score. We will need to have a short, quick, arm action to throw the ball, not a winding up motion. What is important here isn't the amount of velocity we put on the ball but how quickly we get it out of our hand! Therefore, we want to throw it like a dart. "Throwing it like a dart" means we should throw the ball with a very short arm action that isn't much more than a flip of the wrist and elbow–just like you would throw a dart!

Make a Good Throw

First we must determine what constitutes a good throw. A good throw is a throw that allows the pitcher to catch the ball easily and apply the tag to the runner who is trying to score. Unlike throws to first, second, or third base, a ball that is thrown knee

The Complete Guide for Baseball Catchers

high is a very difficult throw for the pitcher to handle. We should try to throw the ball at least waist high so the pitcher has no problem catching it.

Throw it like a dart with hips and shoulders square to our target.

The reason we should try to throw it at least waist high is because this is a very difficult play for the pitcher for a number of reasons. First, the pitcher has to run 60 feet from the mound to cover home plate. Because of that distance, the pitcher will usually be getting to home plate around the same time the play is going to be made. He won't be able to stand, stationary, waiting on the throw. Second, there is a base runner sliding into home plate, so a low throw is going to be very difficult for a pitcher to catch when he has a runner coming at him with his spikes up! Last, this play isn't practiced very often by pitchers because of its infrequency. Giving them a challenging throw is only going to lower the chances that we actually tag the runner out before he crosses home plate.

Chapter 11

Pitchouts

A pitchout is when we or the coaches have a strong feeling that the other team is going to attempt a stolen base and we are willing to intentionally throw a ball outside the strike zone to give us a better chance to throw the base runner out. Our odds of throwing the base runner out will greatly increase, so we are willing to throw a ball to the batter in exchange for an out on the base paths. However, if we guess wrong and the runner doesn't attempt to steal, we have essentially wasted a pitch. But a pitchout can be a great tool if used at the right time!

How do you know when to call a pitchout? There are a few situations when we may choose to do this. First, we have a good scouting report on the other team, we know their tendencies, and we know which counts they like to steal in. A lot of teams are creatures of habit, and they have rules or guidelines that tell them to run when possible and when a certain base-stealing runner is on base. Pay close attention to this, because it may help you predict when the other team is going to run! Also, many base runners give themselves away because they act differently when they are going to steal and when they're not. Some runners will get jumpy, and it is obvious that they're going to steal. On the other end of the spectrum, there are runners who try to be so nonchalant that they give themselves away by being too relaxed. A trained eye will help you determine these two types of base runners and, with experience, you will become better at reading them. Even if you're not playing, you can learn a lot by paying attention to the base runners while you're on the bench.

Pitchout to an LHH.

Once we have given the pitchout signal to our pitcher, we should set up in our secondary stance on the outside half of the plate (this will be different for RHH and LHH). Once the pitcher breaks his hands and his front knee and foot start to descend, we should take a jab step into the outside batter's box. We should be far enough outside that the pitcher is sure to throw it where the batter cannot make contact with the pitch. We should also remain in an athletic position, balanced and with our knees slightly bent, so that we can react to a poorly located pitchout. The pitcher should see our mitt in the middle of our chest. As we are about to receive the pitch, we should let our momentum take us slightly forward. This will allow us to throw the ball to second base more quickly, and we will have an advantage over the base stealer.

It is not necessarily a bad thing if the runner doesn't attempt to steal. Showing the opposing team that we are willing to pitchout

CATCHING-101

may cause them to be more hesitant about stealing and may prevent them from stealing in the future.

On a side note, we do not want our pitcher to slide step to the plate on a pitchout, because the runner may not steal if he sees the pitcher take a shorter leg lift. The pitcher should deliver the four-seam fastball to home plate at the same speed or slightly faster so that it does not throw up a red flag to the base runner.

Pitchout to an RHH.

Chapter 12

Intentional Walks

There are certain situations in a baseball game when it may benefit our team to intentionally walk a batter. We may choose to walk a batter because he is the best player on the other team or the hottest hitter at the time, and we would rather take our chances facing the next batter. An example would be Barry Bonds in 2001, the year he hit 73 homeruns and was walked 177 times. Maybe there is only one out with runners on second and third base, with the runner on third being the winning run. We need a double play to end the inning, so we decide to walk the batter, hoping we can get the next batter to ground into a double play.

A lot of youth leagues allow catchers to intentionally walk a batter by simply telling the umpire that they want to issue an intentional walk. However, at higher levels of baseball, we must actually throw four balls in order for the batter to walk. This makes it a little more difficult because now the pitcher could possibly make a bad throw that either gets hit or goes to the backstop.

When we are issuing an intentional walk, or intentional base on balls (IBB), we want to give the pitcher a good target and be in an athletic position, ready to receive an errant throw. We should set up on the outer half of the plate, standing with our knees slightly

CATCHING-101

Intentionally walking an LHH.

bent. If we are intentionally walking an LHH, our left arm should be extended into the right-handed batter's box, giving the pitcher a target that is well outside the strike zone. When we are intentionally walking an RHH, we should extend our right arm into the left-handed batter's box. As the pitcher is releasing the ball, we should shuffle our feet so that we are in the middle of the batter's box opposite the hitter. Hopefully, our pitcher will deliver a fastball that will hit us in the chest, but we need to be prepared for a wild throw.

The Complete Guide for Baseball Catchers

Intentionally walking an RHH.

Chapter 13

Backing up First Base

When a ground ball is hit to the infield, catchers should back up throws to first base in order to defend an overthrow or a ball thrown in the dirt to the first baseman. When there are no runners on base, we should back up first base every time there is a ball hit to the infield. Sometimes we will back up first base even when there are runners on base. If there is a possible double play ball hit (with a runner on first only), we should still run to back up first so that an overthrown ball doesn't go into the dugout or out of play.

When we run to back up first base, we want to put ourselves in a position where we could field a poorly thrown ball. With that said, we do not always run to the same position behind first. We should line ourselves up with first base and where the ball was fielded. For example, if a ball is hit to the second baseman, an overthrown ball will not end up in the same place it would have if the ball was hit to the third baseman. Generally, we won't have to run as far to back up a ball hit to the second baseman as we will a ball hit to the shortstop. And we will have to run farther on a ball hit to the third baseman than we would on a ball hit to the shortstop.

It is also important that we give ourselves enough room behind the first baseman to be able to field the errant throw. If we are too

The Complete Guide for Baseball Catchers

close to the first baseman, it will be hard to field the ball cleanly. Likewise, we shouldn't be too close to the fence or dugout because we don't want the ball to go out of play if we misplay the ball. Therefore, we should find a happy medium between the first baseman and the fence or dugout.

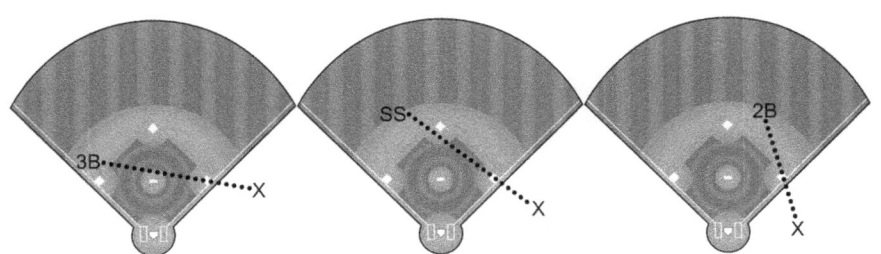

Correct area to be in when backing up a throw to first base.

When a ball gets past the first baseman, the runner will often make a turn toward second base, thinking he can advance another base. So we must be ready to throw the ball to second or to make the play at first base. If the runner makes his turn toward second base, we can tag him with the ball, and he will be out, so be aggressive and try to tag him if he does make a turn.

Chapter 14

Full Arm Fake

There are a few times when we will want to make a full arm fake (fake throwing to a base), and it is important that we do a good job or we won't fool the base runners.

The three most common plays that call for a full arm fake are first and third situations, 1-2-3 double plays, and bunt plays. Some teams have plays for first and third situations that call for the catcher to full arm fake to second base and then throw to third base. In order to get the runner on third base to take a significant lead off the base, we must fool him into thinking we're going to throw the ball to second base. When the bases are loaded and there are less than two outs, we could possibly have a 1-2-3 double play. If the ball is hit back to the pitcher and he is going to throw it to us for the first out, we may be able to throw it to first base for the second out. However, if the runner is too fast and we're not able to throw him out, we may want to full arm fake to first base and look to third base to see if the runner rounding third took too big a turn. Another time when we are most likely to full arm fake is after a bunt with a runner on second base. If the batter makes a good bunt and we can't throw him out at first base, we should full arm fake instead of just holding on to the ball. We might fool the runner rounding third base into taking a bigger turn and getting far enough off the base so that we can pick him off. Even if we don't fool the runner, it's OK. We don't have anything to lose by trying!

The key to a believable full arm fake is having an exaggerated follow-through. The most common mistake players make when giving full arm fakes is that they rush through it and shorten up their arm action so it is not believable. Do not rush! Give the play time to develop. We want it to look realistic, so our arm action must be the same as if we were really going to throw the ball.

We have two options when it comes to the full arm fake: keep the ball in our mitt or hold the ball in our hand. Each method has pros and cons, so you'll need to decide which one you prefer. By keeping the ball in our mitt, we are less likely to lose control of the ball; we're not faking the throw with the ball in our hand and running the risk of losing our grip and letting go of the ball. However, it isn't going to look believable if the ball isn't in our hand, so we may not fool the runner. You do risk the possibility of losing the ball if you full arm fake with the ball in your hand, but it definitely looks more realistic. If you feel comfortable full arm faking with the ball in your hand, go for it. But if, during practice, you have accidentally let balls slip and get away from you, it might be a good idea to full arm fake with the ball in your mitt.

Just like with any of our other skills, we can improve our full arm fake–but it takes practice. We should work on this whenever we practice fielding bunts. After we have gotten enough repetitions throwing to first, full arm fake to first base, and then throw to third base.

Chapter 15

Knowing the Field

One thing unique to catching is that we must be more familiar with the field than any other player is. By this I mean that we must really know our surroundings, including the ground rules. If the ground rules are not posted in the dugout, you should ask your coach what they are before the game. The ground rules that are particularly helpful for catchers to know include whether the top step of the dugout is live or dead and if there are any areas around the backstop that are dead. One example is that if the ball enters the designated area for bat boys it is a dead ball.

Backstop

Before each game, we should take a few minutes to look around the field and take in the surroundings. We should notice what the backstop is made of. If it is made of brick, we should realize that a pass ball or wild pitch is going to deflect much more quickly than if the backstop is padded or is a chain link fence. Take a few balls and throw them against the backstop to see how they react when they hit. Do they jump off, or do they die?

Warning Track

Is there a warning track? If there is a warning track and we attempt to slide for a pass ball or wild pitch, we will slide differently than we would if we were sliding on grass or artificial turf. How wide is the warning track? Sometimes they are only a few feet from the fence, while other times they could be up to 10 feet wide.

Dugouts

We should also realize how far the dugout extends down the line. We need to know this because if an infielder overthrows the first baseman, we need to know if the ball is going to deflect off the fence or wall or possibly go into the dugout. This might change the angle we take when backing up first base.

Baselines

Another thing we can learn before the game is how bunts roll. Some fields are crowned so that bunts down the line seem to roll foul often, while other fields are very flat so that bunts down the line roll very true. Before the game, possibly during infield/outfield, we should take a few balls with us to home plate and roll them down the first and third base lines to see how they roll. This can be helpful to us during the game when we are trying to make split second decisions about whether to let the ball roll foul or whether to field the ball and throw the runner out.

Weather

Also, we should know the conditions of the field and how they affect play. For example, if the field is wet because of rain, it is usually a good day to throw runners out who are attempting to steal. As a base runner, it is harder to get a good jump on a wet field than on a dry one. Again, if it is wet outside, we are more

CATCHING-101

likely to slide farther when attempting to get pass balls or wild pitches, so we should keep that in mind. When the field is really dry, it usually plays faster, so throws coming from the outfield that bounce will generally be faster and stay lower to the ground.

Foul Territory

Some fields have more foul territory than others. We need to know this for pop flies and for pass balls or wild pitches. On fields with very little room between home plate and the backstop, runners are less likely to attempt to score on a ball that gets by the catcher. On the other hand, we are more likely to be able to catch pop flies in foul territory on fields that have a lot of room inside the fences.

Ground Rules

We should know the ground rules of our home field, and we should ask the coach what the ground rules are when we are playing on the road. For example, we need to know if the top step of the dugout is in play or dead. It would be foolish to miss an out because we are unaware of the ground rules.

Chapter 16

Pre-Game Infield/Outfield

There are a few important things to accomplish during pre-game infield/outfield. It is also crucial to remember that we can get very good work in during infield/outfield, as opposed to just going through the motions.

We should always have our arms completely loose before taking infield/outfield. If you have a sore arm, ask your coach if you need to take it. As a coach, I do not require our catchers to take it every day, but your coach may have a different policy. Even if you choose not to throw, there are certain things we can do during infield/outfield.

The first thing I like our catchers to do during infield/outfield is to roll balls down the first and third base lines to see how they roll. Every field is different, and some surfaces act a certain way. For instance, on some fields balls that are bunted down the third base line tend to stay in fair territory, while on other fields a ball bunted in the same spot will tend to roll into foul territory. It is good to know this information before the game so that we can feel confident with our split second decisions during the game.

The next thing we want to do during infield/outfield is to examine home plate. Different plates tend to have different qualities. These could include the plate being either soft, hard,

CATCHING-101

slippery, or raised. It is especially important to know if the plate is slippery so that we can position ourselves not to step on it, especially if we are wearing plastic or molded spikes.

Last, but most important, we have to take the throws from the outfield very seriously. This may be the only chance we have to see how thrown balls react off the surface. For example, on some fields balls thrown from the outfield may tend to skip hard and low, and we need to be prepared for this in the event of a play at home plate. Other fields may react differently, and the ball may check up or bounce higher and lose speed after it hits the ground. Field conditions may also play a role in this. How will the ball react if the field is very wet? How will the ball react if the field is very dry? These are important questions to ask ourselves before the game starts. If we go into the game unprepared and uninformed, it may cause us to make mistakes that could have been easily prevented by taking infield/outfield more seriously.

Chapter 17

Giving Catchers Accurate Feedback

Evaluating catchers and giving them accurate feedback is one of the most important things coaches can do. Sometimes the feedback isn't great, but the sooner we learn to accept constructive criticism, the more we will really grow as a catcher. Coaches, know that when we allow a catcher or any player to do something incorrectly and we do not correct them, we are reinforcing that their actions were acceptable or correct. Catchers, your coaches, parents, and instructors want you to become better and to improve your skills! If they are giving you constructive criticism, it is because they are trying to help you. Be open-minded about trying new things that will help you get where you want to be.

With today's technology, it is easier than ever to give catchers an accurate evaluation. Here are two things every catcher should take advantage of:

Video Evaluation

One of the major advances in technology for the baseball world is video review software. Systems like RightView Pro and Dartfish provide an excellent way to evaluate pitching or hitting mechanics, and I recommend them to anyone who has the resources to buy one. However, you don't need an expensive video system to benefit from watching video. I'd be willing to bet that most of you reading this have a video camera on a cell phone or camera that you keep with you! Use it to take video of yourself or your catchers to see exactly what you or they are doing correctly or incorrectly.

More than 65% of people are visual learners, and baseball players are no exception. With video we can really speed up the learning curve by reinforcing what we're teaching. When players see themselves on a TV screen or computer monitor, it is easier for them to understand what a coach or parent is trying to explain.

I strongly recommend that you start keeping a video library of yourself or your catchers that you can reference whenever you want. It's great to have video of yourself when you're doing a good job throwing, blocking, or receiving; you can refer to it when you're not playing your best and make the appropriate adjustments.

Catchers should also take advantage of MLB games on TV. Each of the 30 teams plays 162 regular season games in addition to spring training and postseason games (if they're fortunate). That's a lot of games on TV! If you choose to pay close attention to what is going on during these games, you can learn a lot from the best catchers in the world. Unlike other positions, you can see the catchers during every pitch of the game. Every time they receive a pitch, block a ball, put down signals, or throw a runner out, you get to see it. It's possible to watch an entire game and never see the right fielder catch or throw a ball! You'd be surprised at how much you can learn by watching a Big League game and paying close attention to the catchers. Take advantage of this opportunity to learn from the guys you wish to play with one day!

The Complete Guide for Baseball Catchers
Catcher's Performance Summary

Catchers usually do not get enough accurate feedback about their defensive performance. A typical evaluation of a catcher might say "good receiver" or "bad at blocking." The evaluations are generally very vague, and catchers often don't know exactly how well or how poorly they're doing at receiving, blocking, or pitch calling. One way to help catchers improve is to give them more detailed and accurate feedback by keeping a Catcher's Performance Summary.

Both hitters and pitchers have access to more statistics than you can imagine, but catchers are usually left out. For example, if you watch a Major League game on TV, you may hear the announcers say what a pitcher's ERA is when pitching in a dome, what a hitter's batting average is against left-handed pitchers during day games, or maybe even what a hitter's batting average is during his third at bat! The list goes on and on, but you never hear how many times a catcher had to block a ball thrown in the dirt during a game. Why not? Wouldn't it be beneficial to know how often a catcher blocks a ball in the dirt or drops a pitch that hits his mitt? I think so, and that's why I keep a Catcher's Performance Summary.

A Catcher's Performance Summary should be kept to report on a catcher's defensive statistics. There are a few options for creating this report. You can use one similar to the one I've put in this book, make your own, or use the Catcher's Performance Summary app for iPhone, iPad, and iPod Touch. The most important thing is to show the catcher exactly how he is performing in games, not how you keep his chart.

Catchers need to be made aware of the number of balls they're blocking, the number of balls they drop, the number of pass balls or wild pitches being thrown, and the number of runners caught stealing, as well as their pop times throwing to bases and their Catcher's Earned Run Average (CERA). These are just a few of

CATCHING-101

the important statistics that a catcher needs to know in order to focus on areas that need improvement.

These numbers are valuable for coaches as well as catchers. Having this information may help coaches make better decisions about which catcher gets the most playing time. For example, the average number of blocks a catcher makes per game (Blocks/9 Innings) tells us a few things. First, catchers who block more balls per nine innings are generally better at blocking. Maybe this is because they have better mechanics, or maybe they can read a ball in the dirt quicker than the other catchers on the team can. Aside from being a better blocker, catchers who block more balls per game usually are more trusted by their pitchers. When pitchers throw more balls in the dirt to one catcher than another, it is probably because they trust that the catcher will not let the ball get to the backstop. So, if you dig a little deeper, knowing how many balls your catcher is blocking will tell you a lot about what the pitching staff really thinks of him! And that is just one example of how statistics can let you know a lot more about your catcher.

I think the best way to keep these statistics is by using the app for iPhone, iPad, or iPod Touch–probably because I developed it! These stats don't mean a thing if you don't make the catcher aware of his performance. Using the CPS app allows you to view and email the statistics by choosing a catcher and the date range for which you want to see his stats and then clicking "Generate Report". The app lets you email your catcher his stats immediately after the game, while it is still fresh in his mind. After each game, I like to email my catchers two reports: one with their most up-to-date season statistics and one with statistics from the game just played.

Even if you don't use the Catcher's Performance Summary app, I would encourage you to keep a paper copy like the one provided in this book. If catchers aren't made aware of their strengths and weaknesses, it is going to be hard for them to improve as baseball players.

CATCHING-101
Catcher's Performance Summary

Name:_____

Date:_____

Pitchers Caught:_____
_____

Total # of Innings:_____

# of Steal Attempts:_____

# of Runners Thrown Out:_____

# of Pass Balls/WPs:_____

# of Blocks:_____

# of Drops:_____

Pop Times to 2B:_____

Helped in Bullpen? Y   N

Notes:_____
_____
_____
_____

Chapter 18

Communicating with the Umpire

A nine inning ball game is usually lasts between two-and-a-half and three hours. About half time will be spent on defense, and if you communicate well with the home plate umpire, that time can be much more enjoyable. That doesn't mean you have to become best friends with him, but by communicating with the umpire you can often help your team win, not because he is going to give you favorable calls, but by learning his strike zone and his tendencies and using that knowledge to your advantage.

The first time you jog out to home plate, you should make it a habit to introduce yourself and shake the umpire's hand. If it's the first time you've worked with that umpire, make a point to remember his name! If you're a youth player and don't feel comfortable addressing an umpire by first name, then "Sir" is completely acceptable. However, studies have shown that people respond best to their own name, so I encourage you to use his name when speaking to any umpire.

When speaking with umpires and others, honesty is the best policy. If an umpire asks for your feedback, you should tell him the truth. Sometimes umpires will make a ball or strike call and then ask you what you thought about it. If you agree with them, you should let them know, and if you disagree with the call, you should let them know in a respectful way. "I thought it was a

CATCHING-101

strike" is not always the correct answer! After all, umpires are human and they will make some mistakes.

If you believe that an umpire missed a call, it is OK to let him know if you do it the right way. No one wants to be constantly corrected, but occasionally saying, "I thought that was a pretty good pitch. Did you think it was low or outside?" will help you learn his strike zone. You could also respond by saying, "I think we've gotten that pitch earlier in the game."

These are ways to let the umpire know that you believe he missed a pitch and still be respectful.

Work to have a great relationship with the umpires you work with.

Everyone likes to get positive feedback and hear from someone when they do something well. Umpires are no different! If you think an umpire called a great game, be sure to let him know. I'm sure no umpire would admit to it, but you might get a borderline call go in your favor if you're respectful and enjoyable to be around!

It is never a good idea to talk badly about an umpire in front of another one, even if they clearly missed a call. For example, if you make a great throw to second base and it looks like the base stealer is out but the field umpire calls him safe, there is no need to make a comment to the home plate umpire. You wouldn't want to hear someone make a negative comment about one of your teammates, and umpires feel the same way. Keep the negative comments about other umpires to yourself!

If you're looking for an ice breaker to start conversation with an umpire, you might try one of these:

"Where are you from?"
"When/where is the next game that you umpire?"
"We couldn't have asked for better weather today!"
"What is your favorite ballpark to umpire in?"
"Which is the best team you've seen this year?"
"Have you ever called a no-hitter or a perfect game?"

Chapter 19

Being Vocal on the Field

One quality that every catcher should have is the ability to be loud and vocal on the field. A unique thing about being a catcher is that you can see every other fielder and all the base runners at all times. Therefore, we have to be decisive and make decisions about which base the ball should be thrown to and communicate that with the rest of our team. If we don't use our voice to let the rest of the team know what we want, they may throw the baseball to the wrong base or maybe not even throw it at all!

Not every player is naturally loud, but that doesn't mean you can't practice your communication skills and improve them just as you would practice any other area of your game. When you're practicing or scrimmaging, work on yelling so everyone in the ballpark can hear you. You may have to come out of your comfort zone to do this, but it could help save your team a few runs over the course of a season.

The higher the level of baseball you play, the less important it may be to be vocal, although that doesn't mean you still shouldn't communicate and direct other players. For example, if you have the chance to play in the Big Leagues, there will be tens of thousands of people at games, and the stadium noise will be very loud. Though you may yell as loud as you possibly can, other infielders won't always be able to hear you; of course, you would

The Complete Guide for Baseball Catchers

expect that Major League baseball players know which base they should throw the ball to. Most amateur players won't have to deal with stadiums that loud, so communicate very loudly what you want your other fielders to do.

Chapter 20

Warming Up Before a Practice or Game

When warming up before a practice or game, there are a few things we want to accomplish. First, and most obvious, is that we want to get loose. A lot of guys don't take this time seriously enough, and they put themselves at a higher risk of getting injured and possibly not playing as well as they could. Take your stretching seriously, and be sure you warm up your muscles before exercise.

Second, every day that we throw, we should at least throw 120 feet, which is close to the distance from home plate to second base on a regulation size field. We can't expect ourselves to be able to throw that distance if we haven't thrown at least that far before the practice or game starts. There will definitely be days when we will long toss and throw much farther than 120 feet, but even on our light throwing days, we should at least back it up to 120 feet. It is unrealistic to only throw 90 feet before a game starts and then expect to make a quality throw of more than 120 feet the first time a base runner tries to steal second base.

Aside from throwing, we can also get quality repetitions by practicing receiving the ball. If you catch the ball with purpose every time your partner throws it to you and work on the things covered in the Receiving chapter, you can get an extra 50 plus reps per day! Over the course of a season and a career, these add up quickly. We can easily work on catching the ball in the sweet spot of the mitt, beating the ball to the spot, and catching the ball with the angle of our mitt staying constant. Why not work on these things as opposed to catching the ball without a purpose? It doesn't take any extra effort, and it will help you become better at receiving the baseball–which is the most important thing we do!

Last, this is a time when we can work on our transfer and develop good habits. Players who have a low transfer on their throws usually transfer the ball low when they're playing catch before a practice or game. The only way to train our body to do something is to do it correctly over and over. We can't expect to be lackadaisical with our transfer during our pre-game routine and then have a great transfer the first time someone attempts to steal second base. We should make a conscious effort to always have a good transfer, whether we're playing catch before a game or we're trying to throw a base runner out stealing a base.

Chapter 21

Signals

Giving Signals

Giving signals to the pitcher is an important job that is often overlooked. The first step is to have a proper signal stance, which we already covered. Next, we want to give deliberate signals that should be easy to see and hard to mistake.

Left: Fastball (1); Right: Curveball (2)

The standard set of signals that most teams will use is 1 for fastball, 2 for curveball, 3 for slider, and 4 (wiggle) for changeup.

The Complete Guide for Baseball Catchers

You do not have to use these signs, but they're pretty standard when no one is on base. If your pitcher throws a pitch other than the four standard ones, we will need a signal for it. Maybe your pitcher doesn't throw a changeup, but he throws a knuckleball instead. 4 (wiggle) might be your signal for the knuckleball.

Left: Slider (3); Right: Changeup (4)

Some pitchers have a hard time seeing the catcher's signals, especially at night. We want to do our best to help the pitcher keep his rhythm and tempo, and his tempo is disrupted if he can't consistently see our signals. If you have a pitcher who can't seem to see the signs as often as he should, try using White Out on your fingers. You can either paint it on your fingernails or on the front of each finger in order to make your fingers more visible to the pitcher. A bottle of White Out is inexpensive, and every catcher should keep one in his bag. Another alternative to White Out is athletic tape. Thin strips of athletic tape between the knuckles seem to work well and don't impair your grip on the ball. If you're out of White Out and athletic tape, try using chalk from the batter's box or foul line. Chalk probably isn't as visible as the first two options, but it's better than nothing.

In the event that you and your pitcher do get crossed up on signals, call time out and jog out to the mound to talk to him and find out what the problem is. The purpose of the mound visit isn't to show your pitcher up or make him look bad, but to find out what is causing the miscommunication and fix the problem. It is frustrating when you get crossed up by a pitcher, but try to keep positive body language. He will appreciate it!

Aside from pitches, there are also many other signals a catcher may give to a pitcher. Some of these include pickoffs, pitchouts, slide steps, and fake shake offs, and there can be many more, depending on how complex your pitching system is. A great time to practice giving your signals is during a pitcher's bullpen session. Ask for the pitchers to give you comments about your signal giving.

Sometimes catchers will call plays, too, like a bunt defense or a first and third defense. It's good to get into the habit of letting all the fielders know when the leadoff batter is hitting. We can do this by stepping out in front of home plate and tapping the top of our helmet and shouting, "Top!" This keeps your fielders in the game mentally and lets them know where the opposing team is in the batting order.

Signs with a Runner on Second Base

When there is a runner on second base, catchers want to give a series of signals to the pitcher so that the opposing team doesn't know which pitch is being thrown. If the runner knows which pitch is coming, he could relay a signal to the hitter or make a more informed decision about when to steal third base. If the runner knows that a curveball is going to be thrown, he may decide to steal, since it is easier to steal on an off-speed pitch than on a fastball.

Before the game, it is best for you and the starting pitcher to determine which set of signals are to be used that day, especially if you have more than one set of signals that you commonly use.

The Complete Guide for Baseball Catchers

Avoid waiting for a runner to reach second base before you speak to the pitcher about this. That can disrupt a pitcher's tempo, and it also shows other teams and coaches that you're not organized or possibly that you don't have your head in the game. Be sure to do the same for relievers. Let them know which signs to use when a runner is on second base before you're ever in that situation.

We should pay attention to the runner at second base and try to determine if he is stealing our signs. If he is, we need to visit the mound and let our pitcher know that we need to use a different set of signs. If the runner has our signs, he may relay them to the batter using "open hand/closed hand." If he makes fists with his hands, he may be signaling that a fastball is coming. If the runner leaves his hands open, he may be signaling that an off-speed pitch is going to be thrown. Another thing he may do is tip the location by turning his head. If the runner looks toward the second base bag, he could mean that the pitch is being thrown away from an RHH or inside to an LHH. If he looks to the third base side of the field, he may be saying that a pitch is being thrown inside to an RHH or outside to an LHH. We should be aware of what the runner is doing and change our signs if we think that the opposing team knows them.

There are a few common series that teams will use, but I would encourage you to come up with your own system that no one else knows. For these examples we will say that 1 = Fastball, 2 = Curveball, 3 = Slider, and 4 = Changeup.

Hot Sign

Before the game starts, we can determine that the second sign given tells which pitch is going to be thrown. You could use the first sign, last sign, third sign, or whatever else you choose. Let's say that our signal with a runner on second base is going to be the second sign. If the catcher gives the pitcher the series "3, 2, 2, 1,

CATCHING-101

4," it would mean that he wants a curveball (2) to be thrown. Still using the second sign, the sequence "4, 1, 3, 2, 1" would be the signal for a fastball (1).

This can be a good system to use because it is easy for the pitcher to decipher, but it is easy for the runner at second base to decipher, too. I recommend that if you're using it, you should try to include your signal more than once in the sequence. For example, if my pitcher and I are using the third signal and I give "3, 2, 3, 1, 1," the runner may not know if the first "3" or the third "3" was the real sign.

This system is used a lot after the pitcher shakes off. Maybe you and your pitcher are using a more complex set of signs, and he shakes you off. Instead of going through the entire complex set of signs again, you may tell your pitcher that you are going to use the first or second sign if he shakes you off. If you're not on the same page, doing that may help your pitcher keep his rhythm and tempo by saving time.

First Sign after the "2"

Another common system that teams will use is the First Sign after the "2." This means that "2" is the indicator, and the next signal after a "2" is the pitch. For example, if the catcher gives "2, 1, 3, 4, 4," he wants to throw a fastball (1), because it was the first signal after "2." "3, 1, 1, 2, 2" would mean that the catcher is calling for a curveball (2). The indicator doesn't have to be the number "2," but that is what a lot of teams will use. It could be the first sign after "1," if that's what you designate it to be.

Ahead, Behind, Even

This is a slightly more complex system requiring that a pitcher and catcher have a lot of game awareness or they could get crossed up easily. The catcher will give three signals every pitch, and the indicator is the count on the hitter. If the pitcher is ahead in the count, it would be the first signal. If the pitcher is behind in the count, it would be the second signal. An even count would be the third and last signal. For example, if the count is 0-2 on the hitter (which means that the pitcher is ahead) and the catcher gives "2, 1, 4," then the catcher would be calling for a curveball (2). If the catcher were to give "2, 1, 4" again when he is behind in the count (let's say there is a 3-1 count), he would want a fastball (1). If the count is even, 1-1, he would be asking for a changeup (4).

This system is a little more complex than some of the others, but that also makes it harder to steal by an opposing team.

Outs + 1

Similar to the Ahead, Behind, Even system, with Outs + 1 the catcher will always give three signals, and the indicator is the number of outs plus one. If there are zero outs, the signal would be the first one that the catcher puts down (0 + 1 = 1, first signal). If there are two outs, the third signal would be the indicator (2 + 1 = 3, third signal). For example, let's say there is one out and the catcher gives "2, 3, 1." He would be calling for a slider (3) because 1 out + 1 means that the second signal was the pitch the catcher wanted.

Another variation of this would be Strikes + 1. In this case, because the signal can change multiple times during an at bat, it would take extreme focus between both the catcher and the pitcher so that no one gets crossed up. I only recommend using a system this complicated for very advanced baseball players.

Indicator System

One popular system that teams use is called the Indicator System. This is where the first signal the catcher gives to the pitcher is the indicator for the following signs. If the first signal the catcher gives is a "1," then the first signal following that would be the hot sign. If a catcher were to give a "3" for the first signal, the hot signal would be the third sign that follows. Here are a few examples: If the catcher were to give the series "2, 2, 1, 3, 4," he would be calling for a fastball (1), because it is the second signal after the indicator of "2." If you were to give this series to your pitcher "1, 4, 4, 2, 1, 3," you would be calling for a changeup (4), because that is the first signal after the indicator of "1."

Pump System

Some programs will use what is known as a Pump System. The pitcher will count the number of different signs that you put down without necessarily paying attention to what they are. Let's say that our pump system is: 1 pump = changeup, 2 pumps = fastball, 3 pumps = slider, and 4 pumps = curveball. In this example, if we want to call a fastball, we can give the pitcher "1, 2," or "3, 3," or even "4, 2," because each of these series has two separate pumps. If we wanted to call a curveball, we could put down any four signs because 4 pumps = curveball. The series "2, 1, 3" would call for a slider because it is three separate numbers and 3 pumps = slider.

Tap System

Another system that you might see if you watch MLB games is called the Tap System, sometimes referred to as the Touch System. The Tap System is when a catcher will give signals to the pitcher by tapping different areas of his body instead of using the traditional numbers between his legs. The catcher may tap the top of his helmet, his face mask, his chest protector, his cup, or either knee. Each part of the body will represent a particular pitch. For example, the most common signals are face mask = breaking ball, chest protector = changeup, right knee = fastball away from an RHH, and the left knee = fastball inside to an RHH.

The Complete Guide for Baseball Catchers

This is most commonly used in conjunction with the hot sign system, but can be used with any of the systems where a body part replaces a number. We should talk to our starting pitcher before the game and decide which tap we will use. For example, if we are using the third tap and we go through the series: chest, right knee, chest, face mask, and left knee, then the pitch we would be calling for is the changeup (chest). If we are using the second tap and we go through the series chest, face mask, right knee, left knee, and chest, then we would be calling for a breaking ball (face mask).

This system is used so that the signals are clearly visible to the pitcher. Sometimes, when the lighting is poor, it is hard for pitchers to see the signals between our legs, and this could cause us to get crossed up. The Tap System ensures that the pitcher doesn't mistake which signal we give him and should prevent any miscommunications.

These are just a few examples of what catchers can do with runners on second base. Some of these systems can be fairly complex and confusing to pitchers so they should be practiced in the bullpen. You want to be confident that you know which pitch the pitcher is going to throw at all times. It doesn't feel very good to be wondering if the pitcher got the right signal!

It is also the catcher's responsibility to let the middle infielders know which system they are using that day so that they can shift appropriately. It is best to do this before the game starts so they are never caught wondering which pitch is being thrown.

Chapter 22

Catching Wristband

A popular trend in the last few years is for coaches to signal a three or four digit code to the catcher, who will then decipher a legend that he is wearing as a wristband to see which pitch the pitching coach wants. Many coaches have started doing this because it is easy for the catcher but extremely difficult for opposing teams to figure out. The only way an opposing team could break our code would be to write down each series of numbers the pitching coach gives to the catcher and try to reference it for repeats.

The pitching coach will have the bottom portion of the example sheet on a clipboard in the dugout, and the catcher will be wearing the top portion in his wristband. The table in this book is only a template, but a similar one can be made using a computerized spreadsheet program. To decrease the chances of an opposing team stealing our signs, we could have multiple charts that we use on different days.

Example: The pitching coach wants a fastball away, so he gives the catcher the hand signals "0, 1, 1." The first two numbers (0, 1) refer to the two-digit headings on each column on the catcher's wristband. He looks for "01" and sees that it is the first column, in this case. Then he reads the third digit (1) and looks for the row with that number on the left-hand side. The box in column

The Complete Guide for Baseball Catchers

one, row one reads "FBA" which means fastball away. The catcher can then give the pitcher the signal for fastball away.

If the pitching coach gives the hand signals "2, 1, 2," the catcher should call a curveball.

If the pitching coach gives the hand signals "3, 1, 4," the catcher should call a changeup.

	01	02	03	04	05	11	12	13	14	15	21	22	23	24	25
1	FBA	SL	FBA	FBA	FBI	CH	SL	P	P	CB	CH	FBI	FBA	FBA	SL
2	FBI	CB	SL	CH	P	FBI	FBI	FBA	CH	CH	CB	SL	CB	FBI	P
3	FBA	CB	P	CH	CB	FBA	FBI	CH	P	SL	CB	FBA	FBA	FBI	CH
4	CB	FBI	FBI	P	CH	FBA	SL	CB	CB	CH	P	CH	FBI	SL	CB
5	SL	FBI	FBA	SL	FBA	CH	CH	CB	SL	FBI	FBA	FBA	SL	P	CH

	31	32	33	34	35	41	42	43	44	45	51	52	53	54	55
1	SL	FBA	SL	FBI	FBA	CH	SL	FBA	SL	FBI	P	CH	CH	FBI	FBA
2	P	SL	CB	FBA	SL	CB	CB	FBA	CH	P	FBA	FBI	CH	SL	CB
3	CH	CH	CB	FBI	CB	FBA	SL	FBI	CH	CB	FBI	CB	SL	FBI	FBA
4	CH	CB	FBI	FBA	CB	FBA	CH	CB	P	CB	FBA	CB	FBA	FBI	FBA
5	FBI	SL	FBA	SL	SL	FBI	P	SL	CH	FBA	CH	SL	FBA	FBA	CB

FBA = Fastball Away

FBI = Fastball In

CB = Curveball

SL = Slider

CH = Changeup

P = Pickoff

FBA		FBI		CB		SL	
011	321	051	341	151	332	021	311
031	351	221	451	022	412	121	331
041	431	012	541	212	422	251	421
231	551	112	521	232	552	032	441
241	342	122	343	023	333	222	322
132	432	242	433	053	353	153	352
013	512	123	513	213	453	124	542
113	413	243	543	015	523	244	423

CATCHING-101

223	553	024	334	134	324	015	533
233	344	034	544	144	354	045	325
114	414	234	315	254	434	145	345
035	514	025	415	135	454	235	355
055	534	155			524		435
215	554				555		525
225	335						
	455						
	535						
	545						

CH		P	
111	411	131	511
211	521	141	312
042	531	052	452
142	442	252	444
152	532	033	425
043	313	143	
133	323	044	
253	443	214	
054	314	245	
154	424		
224	445		
115	515		
125			
255			

Chapter 23

Catching a Ceremonial First Pitch

Many games have what is known as a ceremonial first pitch, when a coach, alumni, donor, or celebrity is honored and is asked to throw out a pitch before the top of the first inning. There is a certain etiquette that should be followed so that it is a great experience for the honoree.

As a token of appreciation, the person who is asked to throw out the ceremonial first pitch will get to keep the ball they threw. So after the person being honored throws the pitch to us and we catch it, we should jog out to them and shake their hand. It's always nice to thank them by saying something like, "Thanks for throwing out the first pitch. We really appreciate everything that you've done," or something similar to that. After you say thanks and shake their hand, hand them the baseball. Then jog back to home plate and begin to catch the starting pitcher's warm ups.

Chapter 24

Catcher's Practice

At this point, we have covered many, many things catchers need to do well to have success. It is important to understand that we must organize our time better than any other player on the field. At each practice, we simply do not have enough time to practice everything we might do in a game. So here is a practice plan that will help catchers allocate their time effectively.

Every day at practice, we should be smart about how we spend our time during the defensive session. The two most important jobs we have–receiving and blocking–should be practiced every day. A day shouldn't go by without a catcher practicing both of these! It's not about catching 1,000 pitches a day, it's about getting high quality repetitions. All athletes have heard the phrase "It's not about quantity; it's about quality." Well that phrase couldn't be more true for catchers. When practicing your receiving and blocking, focus on using proper mechanics and

1. Receiving
2. Blocking
3. Throwing Mechanics
4. Bullpens

Practice the most important things most often!

practicing at game speed.

After we practice receiving and blocking, we should try to practice at least one other skill each day. Some days we will practice receiving, blocking, and tag plays at the plate. Other days we might practice receiving, blocking, and fielding bunts. Because there are so many things to practice, we may have to practice outside of our team's practice schedule. If you feel like you need to hone one of your skills even more, have a dad, brother, teammate, or coach work with you before or after practice.

Catching might be the hardest position on the field, simply because we have so many different skills to practice and there isn't enough practice time to do them all every day. We must practice them all frequently enough to stay sharp and keep our mechanics tight.

Chapter 25

Receiving Drills

As discussed in the chapter Catcher's Practice, we should practice our receiving drills EVERY day we practice. There shouldn't be one practice day when catchers don't practice receiving the ball. Below I've outlined the drills I believe work extremely well and focus on the important aspects of catching.

Ten repetitions per round seems to be a good number to use for all of these receiving drills, except perhaps Quick Hands, which we'll discuss in more detail. There are too many drills for you to do all of them every day, so as a coach or player, you need to decide what will be the emphasis of that day's practice.

We should always wear full equipment when practicing receiving. This includes our face mask! The risk far outweighs the reward of catching without protection on our head, even when we are catching tennis balls, Incrediballs, or balls thrown at a lower velocity.

Receiving Tennis Balls Bare-Handed

Receiving Tennis Balls Bare-Handed is a pretty common drill in the catching world. However, it is quite often done incorrectly. It can be a very good drill when done correctly with an emphasis on the right things. This is a great drill for the beginning of practice and can be used as a warm-up drill.

Our partner or coach should be kneeling about 25 feet away with about 10 tennis balls. The balls should be thrown firmly, but not so hard that they cannot be caught. Balls should be thrown all over the strike zone, not just down the middle of the plate.

The most important aspect of this drill is that we catch the tennis ball in between our index finger and thumb. If we can do this consistently, we will learn to catch the ball in the mitt's sweet spot. Too often players do this drill with good intentions, but they catch the ball in the palm of their hand or the palm of their mitt. Catching the ball in the palm of our mitt will not give us the results we want because balls will consistently pop out. To do this drill correctly, the ball must be caught between the thumb and index finger.

Partner Throws - Short Distance

Partner Throws should be a standard drill that we practice nearly every day. We can do this drill with a partner and 10 baseballs. Our partner could be a coach, teammate, brother, or parent. Our partner will kneel about 15 to 25 feet away and throw balls all over the strike zone. The balls should be thrown well below game speed. We have other drills where we will practice receiving high velocity pitches, but this is not one of them.

We should concentrate on the most basic aspects of receiving in this drill–keeping our bodies quiet and receiving with strong hands. If there is one particular pitch we are having trouble with (inside to an RHH, for example), we should concentrate on working on our weaknesses as we let our partner throw to us. In this drill, one or two rounds of 10 repetitions should be sufficient before we move on to our next receiving drill.

CATCHING-101

This drill isn't supposed to be very difficult; it is just meant to help us work on our receiving mechanics. Drills don't have to be difficult to be effective, as long as we concentrate on working on very specific things like keeping our body quiet, beating the ball to the spot, or maybe catching high pitches deep and receiving low pitches farther out in front of our body. Hitting baseballs off a tee isn't a difficult drill, but it can be a good drill if the player has the right attitude and work ethic. The same holds true for Partner Throws at a Short Distance. This drill is designed to work on improving our receiving mechanics in a very controlled environment, and we should have a high success rate. Our goal in this drill should be to always catch every ball.

Partner Throws - Longer Distance

There are a few differences in Partner Throws at a Short Distance and at a Longer Distance. First, our partner is now standing up and could be 35 to 45 feet away. Our partner should now be throwing the ball with much more velocity, which will make this drill more challenging. The increased velocity will require us to be quicker with our mitt and beat the ball to the spot.

Unlike Partner Throws at a Short Distance, at the longer distance we shouldn't necessarily catch every ball thrown. If our partner is throwing the ball as hard as he should be, we will occasionally miss a pitch. If we do this drill every day over the course of a season and we catch every ball, then it isn't as challenging as it is supposed to be. If we find ourselves catching every pitch over an extended period of time, we should ask our partner to throw it slightly harder. However, if we are missing a ball or two every round, we may find that the drill is too challenging, and our partner should take a little pace off the throws.

Partner Throws at a Longer Distance is a great compliment to Partner Throws at a Short Distance because it transitions the

The Complete Guide for Baseball Catchers

catcher into a more difficult drill such as Quick Hands or Receiving from a Pitching Machine.

Receiving from Pitching Machine

Receiving pitches thrown from a pitching machine is an excellent drill because we can catch a lot pitches thrown at high velocities that are at or above game speed. If you don't have access to a pitching machine, it's OK, but check with your local high school, batting cages, or training facility to see if you can rent or borrow one.

The pitching machine should be set up between 45 and 60 feet away, and the velocity can range from easy to very difficult. Most players won't get the opportunity to catch a pitcher throwing 95 mph, but it is good to practice catching at this speed because we might one day have a pitcher on our team who throws that fast. Receiving balls from a pitching machine will allow us to practice catching balls thrown at 90 mph or more in a controlled environment.

Our partner should be very deliberate about showing us the ball before he places it in the machine. The best thing is for him to hold the ball up where we can see it and then place it in the machine. By doing this, we aren't caught off guard or surprised when the ball is released. Doing this will prevent any accidents due to poor timing.

Although pitching machines are very accurate for the most part, they do not always throw it exactly where we are expecting it. The ball may cut or run, or it may end up in a different location than we expect because of imperfections in the baseball. Balls that are heavy or waterlogged may not fly exactly like a brand-new baseball. Some balls have seams that are low profile, while others have raised seams. This may cause the balls to fly differently, too. So we may think we know exactly where the ball

CATCHING-101

is going to be thrown, but we still need to react to balls that aren't thrown exactly where we expect them.

There are a few different things we can do when receiving balls from a pitching machine. First, we should set up down the middle of the plate and work on receiving pitches thrown down the middle. After we have received pitches in the middle of the plate, we can work on receiving pitches that were thrown inside or outside to an RHH or LHH. To practice receiving pitches thrown away from an RHH, we should move about one foot to our left. Even though the pitch is being thrown in the same spot as before, this will simulate the pitcher missing his spot to our arm side. To practice pitches away from an LHH, we should shift our bodies about a foot to the right of the center of the plate. This will simulate a pitcher who has missed his spot to our glove side. As a catcher, we should try to recognize which pitches are giving us problems and try to work on them, just as a hitter who struggles with curveballs should spend additional time practicing hitting curveballs. Using a pitching machine can help us practice many repetitions of pitches in a particular location.

After we have worked on receiving balls down the middle, to our arm side, and to our glove side, we can practice receiving breaking balls. Some catchers struggle with breaking balls simply because they haven't practiced receiving them enough. Outside of a game or bullpen session, this may be the only chance we have to receive breaking balls. A lot of machines can be set to throw right-handed and left-handed breaking balls!

Another drill we can do with a pitching machine is called the Walkup Drill. This is where we start behind home plate and catch a pitch. After we successfully catch the ball, we take one or two steps toward the machine and receive the next pitch. This decreases the distance between us and the pitching machine, essentially making the pitch seem faster and causing us to have a quicker reaction time. This is an excellent drill for working on beating the ball to the spot! We should never get so close to the pitching machine that we make ourselves vulnerable to injury and aren't able to react quickly.

Quick Hands Drill

The Quick Hands Drill could also be called the Machine Gun Drill because the catcher will have balls rapidly thrown at him, and his job will be to move his mitt as quickly as possible, trying to get to as many balls as possible. It is an excellent drill for getting catchers to move their mitts quickly and build hand speed.

A coach or partner should empty a bucket of balls (more balls leads to greater difficulty) and kneel five to seven feet in front of the catcher, who should be in his primary stance. The thrower will then pick up balls as quickly as possible and toss them to all parts of the strike zone. It can be difficult to control where the ball is going, but with practice it becomes easier.

The drill should move so quickly that the catcher doesn't have enough time to take the ball out of his mitt and deliberately drop it in a pile beside him. He will have to drop it from his mitt into a pile in front of him. Because the drill moves quickly, we may not have time to catch every ball, and that is OK. Our goal should be to catch as many balls as possible and get our mitt to as many other balls as we can. If the catcher has extra time between pitches, it probably means that the drill is moving too slowly. This should be a challenging drill; we want it to move fast!

Receiving Incrediballs

All of the above drills can also be done with Incrediballs, or rag balls. These soft balls are designed for young players to use before they start using a hard ball, but can be excellent for receiving drills. Because the balls are softer than real baseballs, they are much bouncier. This can make them very hard to catch! If Incrediballs aren't caught in the sweet spot of the mitt (between the index finger and thumb), they will often bounce out. Using these balls will teach players exactly where to catch the ball in the mitt because there is much less room for error. If an Incrediball hits the palm, toe, or heel of a catcher's mitt, it will likely bounce out, especially if it is thrown or shot out of a machine at high velocity.

Catching in the Bullpen

One of the most important things a catcher will do during practice is Catching Bullpens. If you ask any catcher, though, it is probably their least favorite part of practice! If we maintain a good attitude about bullpens and understand how beneficial they can be, then we can really start to improve as a catcher. Catching Bullpens is the absolute BEST practice we can get! It's better than doing any receiving or blocking drill; and we should take pride in how we catch in the bullpen.

Why is this the best practice for us? First, it is done at full game speed. The pitcher is throwing at the same speed he will throw in the game, so it is more realistic than any other drill we can do. All the drills we do are great, but in order to really improve, we must do them as quickly as possible-at game speed.

Second, this is the time when we learn our pitchers. Which pitchers have movement on their fastball? Who throws a slider, and who throws a curve? What is each pitcher's best pitch? Who throws a lot of breaking balls in the dirt? Which pitchers can command the inside part of the plate? These are all questions we will answer through experience–experience catching the different pitchers! This valuable information can make the difference between you calling a good game or a great game.

We can also learn a lot about pitching mechanics in the bullpen. This is a book about catching, so why would we want to learn pitching mechanics? Because the more you know about pitchers, the more valuable you'll be behind the plate. A pitcher might need to make a mechanical adjustment in the middle of a game and if you can spot the needed adjustment, you can save your pitching coach a visit to the mound. That doesn't sound like much, but it might help your team win by allowing the pitching coach or manager to wait until later in the game to make a trip. There is only one other person on the team who spends as much time in the bullpen as we do, and that's the pitching coach! Learn as much as you can from him, and it will make you a better catcher.

Another thing to remember about Catching Bullpens is that it is a great drill for practicing all of our stances. A lot of times catchers will catch an entire bullpen in their primary stance, even when the pitcher is throwing from the stretch. We must practice receiving in our secondary stance for two reasons. The first is that it is a great time to strengthen our legs. It takes more strength to squat in our secondary stance than in our primary stance because we are not resting on our heels. Also, it is important for the pitcher to get used to throwing to us in a secondary stance. We don't want to catch every bullpen or every side work in one stance and then show the pitcher a completely different look during the game. We want him to be familiar and comfortable with us in our secondary stance. The pitcher practices throwing out of the stretch and, when he does, we should practice receiving in our secondary stance.

We can also improve our blocking skills in the bullpen. This is the best place to work on our reaction time. We do not know if the pitcher is going to throw the ball in the air or in the dirt, so we must be alert and anticipate a ball in the dirt, particularly when the pitcher is throwing off-speed pitches. If a batter doesn't hit well in batting practice, how is he going to hit well in a game? If a pitcher can't throw strikes in practice, what is going to keep him from walking batters in a game? If a catcher can't block balls in the bullpen, why would the coach believe he can do it in a game?

CATCHING-101

When we take pride in our bullpens and do a good job, we are going to give pitchers confidence in us. This, in turn, will make them comfortable with us behind the plate, and they'll want to throw to us in the game. Every catcher wants pitchers to ask to throw to him!

Chapter 26

Blocking Drills

Just like receiving, blocking should be practiced every day. It is, arguably, the most important thing we can do to help our team. It is also very difficult to do in a game if you haven't practiced it A LOT! All of our blocking drills should be practiced from our secondary stance.

Due to the nature of the drills, we won't practice blocking 85 or 90 mph fastballs because we don't want to get hurt during practice. We will practice blocking balls that are probably half that speed, sometimes a little more. Do not train yourself to move slowly by practicing slowly. Even though you may be blocking a ball that is coming at only 55 mph, you must always move at your top speed! The analogy I use for this is to ask players, "How do runners get faster?" The answer is that they sprint! They do not get faster by jogging at 50% speed around the track; they must move full speed. If we move at half or three-quarter speed, we will not train our bodies to move faster. The same holds true for building bat speed. The only way to build bat speed is to swing quickly every time we hit. Then, over an extended period of time, we will slowly increase our bat speed. The moral of the story is that we must practice at full speed, even though the ball is not thrown at game speed.

CATCHING-101

Sometimes we should practice recovering balls after we have blocked them. During at least one of the drills performed each day, we should practice fielding the blocked ball with a sense of urgency, trying to recover it as quickly as possible. Some days we may want to recover the ball as if there were a runner on first base, and other days we may recover the ball as if there were a runner on second base. Doing that will prepare us to throw out a base runner trying to advance on a ball thrown in the dirt, no matter which base he is on.

Partner Blocking, Straight Ahead

Partner Blocking is the equivalent of Partner Throws for receiving. It should be one of the staples of our blocking routine, and we should practice it almost every day. Rounds of 10 repetitions will cause us to work up a sweat but not be exhausted. The emphasis of this drill is proper mechanics. We want to make sure we haven't fallen into bad habits, such as getting into a poor blocking position, losing our balance, or trying to catch the ball off the bounce instead of letting it hit our chest protector.

Our partner should be kneeling about 15 to 25 feet away and bouncing balls directly behind home plate. Even though we are working on blocking balls directly behind home plate, we should always be ready for a ball thrown to our arm side or glove side by mistake. It shouldn't be an excuse to not block the ball because our partner didn't throw it exactly where we thought he would.

A bad habit some players can get into during this drill is to fall into the same spot because they are expecting the ball to the thrown exactly the same every time. We should always react to the pitch, even if it is slightly to our right or left.

Our partners should throw the ball firmly enough that it requires us to react quickly, but not so quickly that we can't block the pitch. This drill will transition us into higher intensity and faster moving blocking drills while emphasizing great blocking mechanics.

Partner Blocking to Both Sides

Partner Blocking to Both Sides is similar to Partner Blocking Straight Ahead in that our partner will be kneeling about 15 to 25 feet away from us and bouncing balls in the dirt for us to block. However, there is one big difference in these drills. In order to exaggerate the angle of the ball, our partner will now be at a 30 to 45 degree angle to us. So if we are directly behind home plate, our partner will be in line with the second baseman or shortstop, not the pitcher's mound. However, we will want to keep our bodies squared to the pitcher's mound and not to our partner throwing the ball.

When blocking balls to either side, we have to work on two main things: getting out far enough to square the ball up with our chest, and getting around the ball with our body so that we block it back toward home plate. This drill will exaggerate both of these aspects of blocking. To block a ball coming from such an extreme angle, we will have to do a great job getting to it as well as getting around it.

The most important aspect of this drill is where our partner throws it. A good throw will be challenging to block and will require us to work to get behind the ball; a poor throw will not take full advantage of the drill. Our partner should not throw the ball directly at the catcher, but he should throw it where it will bounce outside of the catcher's outside knee. For example, if we are working on blocking our glove side, our partner should be lined up with the second baseman. He will throw the ball so that it bounces outside of our left knee. This will require us to push with our right leg to get our chest behind the baseball and also to create an angle back toward home plate with our body so that the ball doesn't bounce toward the shortstop.

CATCHING-101

This drill is more effective than simply standing directly in front of the catcher and throwing balls to either side, because it requires the catcher to work harder due to the extreme angle.

Blocking Balls from a Pitching Machine

Blocking balls that are thrown by a pitching machine can be a good drill, but there are also some risks that come along with it. Of all the blocking drills we do, this is the most physically taxing. Pitching machines are great because they can consistently throw balls in the same location at a high velocity, but blocking higher velocity balls also makes us prone to the bumps and bruises that come with the position. However, the increased velocity can challenge our quickness and force us to go at game speed.

The pitching machine should be set up between 40 and 60 feet away from the catcher and set to throw balls that will bounce and hit the catcher in the middle of his chest protector. To increase the difficulty of this drill, increase the speed of the pitch.

Initially, the catcher should set up right behind the plate and block balls that are thrown down the middle of the plate. Once we have finished blocking balls down the middle we can block balls to our arm side or our glove side. Instead of moving the machine, our catcher can shift two to three feet to the left or right, which will create the same effect as balls being thrown to either side. For example, if the catcher shifts 2 to 3 feet right of middle, he will have to push with his right leg to block the ball that is on his glove side.

Half and Half

The first few drills we have just gone over are great for developing our blocking mechanics and helping us become fundamentally sound. However, they only work on one aspect of blocking–our mechanics. As we learned in the chapter on Blocking, catchers must learn to anticipate balls thrown in the dirt and react to them quickly. While the first drills are great for developing our form, they don't do much for our reaction, because the catcher knows that every ball is going to be in the dirt and even where it is going to be thrown. Half and Half will work on a catcher's ability to read the trajectory of the ball and react when it is going to be thrown in the dirt.

Half and Half consists of our partner throwing us balls just like in the other drills. However, now our partner will throw half of the balls in the air for us to receive and half of the balls in the dirt for us to block. This should help train our eyes and teach us to react when a ball is thrown in the dirt. Our partner should randomly throw balls in the air and in the dirt. For example, it doesn't benefit us if our partner throws the first ball in the air, the second ball in the dirt, the third ball in the air, the fourth ball in the dirt, etc. We want this to be random so that it is more game-like, because in a game we don't know when the pitcher is going to bounce a ball for us to block.

The key for this drill is for the catcher not to guess but to react! When catchers start to guess, they will drop to their knees to catch a ball thrown in the air or try to catch balls that have already bounced. We should always anticipate the ball being thrown in the dirt and also be ready for a ball that is thrown in the air.

Younger catchers or catchers doing this drill for the first time should be thrown fastballs. With older or more advanced catchers, curveballs can be thrown to increase the difficulty of the drill.

CATCHING-101

Hockey Goalie Drill

The Hockey Goalie Drill is a fun drill that will challenge a player's quickness and also emphasize preventing passed balls and wild pitches. Year after year, this has been a favorite drill of our catchers because it can also be made into a game.

First, we set up a goal that is between six and ten feet wide using fence posts, cones, or bats propped on a fence. The wider the goal, the more challenging it will be. The catcher will set up in the middle of the goal and try to prevent balls from reaching the goal behind him. The partner or coach will stand about 30 feet away and hold five baseballs that will then be thrown rapid fire in an attempt to get them past the catcher. Some balls should be thrown in the dirt and others in the air. The purpose of the drill is to increase the catcher's range and quickness and to stop balls from getting to the backstop in any way possible.

Younger catchers can start out with fewer than five baseballs and a smaller goal. As the player's skill level advances, the goal should be widened, making it more challenging. Also, to increase or decrease the difficulty of the drill, the speed of the ball can be changed.

Chapter 27

Throwing Drills

There are a few common mistakes we want to avoid when practicing throwing to bases. First, players will sometimes start their throwing motion with the baseball in their throwing hand as opposed to their mitt. We want to make sure that we always start with the ball in our mitt, so that we can practice our transfer and quickly acquiring a four-seam fastball grip. Second, catchers often practice throwing to bases without a hitter standing in the batter's box. We want to be sure to practice throwing to all bases when there are batters present. To make it more realistic, have the batter intentionally swing and miss or fake bunt. This way we prepare ourselves for when we have to throw during a game because we will be used to a hitter swinging the bat. Also, catchers usually practice throwing to bases with an infielder or partner standing on the base that they are throwing to. However, in a game situation, the infielder will be running to cover the base from his position, so we must learn to throw to the base, and not to where the infielder is standing. Last, we can add a live base runner into the equation to get the most realistic practice possible. Using live base runners will allow them to practice stealing bases and let us judge the quality of our throws based on the number of runners we throw out.

Using these few guidelines will ensure a quality practice that will translate into good throws during a game when there is a pitcher standing on the mound, a hitter standing in the batter's box, and a base runner trying to advance a base. Simulating these situations will be much more productive than the controlled environment most catchers usually practice in.

Throwing Standing Up

One of the most basic throwing drills is to start standing in an athletic position with our feet placed just like they would be in our secondary stance and the ball already in our mitt in front of our body. This allows the catcher to focus completely on his footwork.

While this isn't exactly what we do during a game, it is a great drill to do in conjunction with other throwing drills. We want to also practice throwing after receiving a pitch, but if we are trying to focus on our footwork, this drill is great for isolating that.

Throwing from Secondary Stance

Another drill we can do is to start in our secondary stance with the baseball in our mitt. We will then go through our footwork and transfer and throw the ball to the infielder. This works on all aspects of our throwing mechanics and allows us to work on our timing. Sometimes, catchers will "cheat" in practice by starting their footwork well before they have received the pitch, in order to appear quicker and to impress the coaching staff. While it looks quicker, it isn't quite as realistic as what will actually happen in a game. Therefore, it can be just as productive to practice throwing to bases by starting with the ball already in our catcher's mitt.

Throwing After Receiving a Pitch

To put it all together, we will squat behind home plate in our secondary stance and have our partner throw balls for us to receive, and then we will throw them to the bases. This will let us work on our secondary stance and our throwing mechanics all at the same time. This is more realistic than the first few throwing drills that we do.

Throwing Three-Fourths Distance to Base

On certain days, we may not want to throw the entire distance to the bases so we will have our partner stand about three-fourths of the way to a base. There are two main reasons we might choose to do this. One is because we want to have a light throwing day because our arm needs rest. Two is because we really want to focus on our footwork and mechanics, and we can do a better job controlling them when we shorten the distance to the bases.

Each of the drills just described can be done at three-fourths distance, and they should be done in conjunction with throwing the full distance. This is a great drill to do in the late part of the season when players are starting to get sore arms or are fatigued. The shortened distance will take stress off the throwing arm but still allow us to focus on quickness and proper mechanics.

Dry Throws on the Foul Line

Without actually throwing a ball, we can use the foul line in the outfield grass to show us what our body is doing during our throwing motion to 2B. Dry Throws are when we go through our throwing mechanics without throwing the ball. There are two ways we can use the foul line: we can start with our toes on it or we can start by straddling it with our feet.

To practice gaining ground and placing our right foot under our chin, we should start with our toes on the foul line. Then we will go through our throwing mechanics and look to see where our feet are. Catchers who spin their body or rotate along the axis running through their head and chest, will notice that their right foot could actually end up behind the foul line! This would be an indicator that we're not doing a good job of gaining ground toward second base on our throw. Players who are doing a good job gaining ground toward second base will notice that their right foot has crossed over the foul line by six to eight inches.

When we straddle the foul line and go through our throwing mechanics, we should finish with both feet on the foul line. This is an indicator that we are exerting all our energy in a line directly to second base. If we finish and neither of our feet are on the line, we are being inefficient with our energy and aren't utilizing all we can (the common mistake is to finish in the right-handed batter's box). Another mistake players often make is that they either land open, when a line from toe to toe would point to the shortstop, or closed, when a line from toe to toe would point to the second baseman. Both of these are mistakes we want to correct. One way we can test ourselves is to do our footwork with our eyes closed. This way we have no way of cheating and our muscle memory will show. We should close our eyes and then go through our mechanics. Once we have finished, we can open our eyes and look to see if both our feet ended up on the foul line. If they haven't, we will need to work to develop proper footwork.

Chapter 28

Drills for Catcher Pop Flies

Catcher Pop Flies can be one of the most fun skills to practice, but they are seldom practiced enough. Be sure to use any combination of these drills to be prepared to catch any pop fly in a game. Also, be sure to practice catching pop flies during the day and at night. We should be used to catching fly balls under the lights, especially if our team often plays night games.

Pop Flies from a Fungo

The most realistic practice a catcher can get catching pop flies is when a coach is standing at home plate and using a fungo to hit balls straight up. This practice is similar to what a lot of teams do at the end of infield/outfield. It is the most realistic practice because the ball has extreme backspin and is coming off an actual bat, just like a ball coming off a batter's bat in a game.

There is only one negative to having a coach hitting pop flies to a catcher, and that is that it is very difficult! Just like any other part of the game, hitting pop flies that go straight up is a skill that needs to be practiced often in order to be mastered. It can be challenging for a coach to maintain consistency in hitting the kind of balls a catcher would field. If our coach isn't great at hitting pop flies to us, that's OK. We just need to find another drill that

CATCHING-101

will give us enough repetitions so that we are prepared for pop flies during a game.

Pop Flies from a Pitching Machine

An alternative to catching fly balls from a fungo is catching fly balls that are shot out of a pitching machine. A pitching machine is a great tool to use to practice catching fly balls because it can consistently shoot balls higher than most people can hit them, and it can accurately shoot them to the same area.

When setting up the pitching machine, make sure it is set to give the ball the proper spin. We wouldn't want to practice catching balls with a spin that is opposite of what we would see off of a batter's bat.

The most basic thing we can do is shoot a ball out of the machine and then catch it. If we want to make the drill more interesting and difficult, we can shoot multiple balls out of the machine with a few seconds between each. If we were to shoot three fly balls with a four or five second delay between them, it would give our catcher enough time to catch the first ball and then locate and catch the second and third balls. This is a fun drill that catchers enjoy doing and it challenges their ability to quickly locate a fly ball and recognize where it is going to land. To be safe, we should give ourselves enough time between fly balls. This should not be a machine gun drill where there is only one or two seconds between each fly ball.

Fouled off Bunts

The momentum of the game can be completely changed if a batter squares around to bunt, pops it up, and we catch it. It's not a play that happens every game, but we want to have practice catching fouled off bunts so we are prepared when the situation arises.

To practice catching fouled off bunts, we should squat behind home plate in our primary or secondary stance while our coach or partner stands in fair territory directly in front of home plate. Our partner will softly lob the ball in the air about 10 to 15 feet and at a distance that requires us to completely stretch out or possibly even dive for the ball. Balls should be thrown toward the first base dugout, third base dugout, and directly behind us.

This drill will work on helping us take an efficient first step toward the baseball and is similar to a drill that an outfielder would do.

Eagle Eye Drill

Another drill catchers enjoy doing is called the Eagle Eye Drill. This is where a catcher will lie face down on the ground so that he can't see the ball when it is hit or shot out of the machine. Once we hear the crack of the bat or the thump of the machine, we will quickly get up, locate the ball, and catch it. It will challenge us to find the ball quickly and sprint to where it is going to land. This is an excellent drill for catchers who have trouble finding pop flies off the bat.

To make the drill even more difficult, we may have our coach scream, "Now!" when he wants us to get up and locate the ball. This could be delayed until the ball is almost at its pinnacle, which would give us very little time to locate the ball and catch it.

Chapter 29

Drills for Plays at Home Plate

We will need to practice tag plays and force plays at home plate. Tag plays can be difficult because the throw is coming from the outfield and we expect it to bounce at least once before we catch it. This is different from force plays at home plate, where we are receiving the throw from an infielder.

Digs - Glove side/Backhand

A warm-up drill that focuses on catching balls thrown in the dirt is called Digs. This is where we will pick, or scoop, balls thrown into the dirt by our partner who is standing or kneeling 15 to 20 feet away. We should start in an athletic stance as if we are receiving a throw from an outfielder.

Our partner will then intentionally throw balls into the ground, and we will practice catching them on the bounce. We should start off fielding short hops, or balls that bounce a short distance in front of us. Short hops look difficult to the untrained eye but are actually fairly easy to field if we practice enough.

The key to fielding any ball thrown in the dirt is to keep our mitt through the path of the ball for as long as possible. This is similar to hitting a baseball. If our bat enters and leaves the path of the ball very quickly, we don't leave ourselves much room for error. However, if we have a flat swing that stays through the zone of the ball, we are more likely to hit it cleanly. The same rule applies to fielding a ball that has already bounced. We want to make sure we work our glove through the path of the ball in a horizontal, not a vertical, movement. When players don't make these plays, it is usually because they try to catch the ball by moving their glove up or down instead of back to front.

After we practice fielding short hops, we should move to long hops. These are also fairly easy to catch, and this is what we would ideally like our outfielders to throw us. This ball could bounce 10 to 15 feet away from us, and we would have plenty of time to read how it bounces.

The most difficult ball to field is the "in between" hop. This is a ball that is not quite a short hop but not quite a long hop either. These are the most difficult balls to catch, usually because we are not sure whether we should be aggressive and field the ball or wait on it and try to turn it into a long hop. Reading these balls has a lot to do with the speed of the throw and how quick the field is playing.

We should have our partner throw us all three types of hops, and we should work on fielding them using our mitt, as opposed to blocking the ball with our body. This is also a drill that a first baseman would do to improve his glove work, catching balls thrown from infielders. Just like a first baseman, we need to practice catching these balls to our forehand and backhand side.

Balls Hit from Fungo

The most effective way to practice fielding tag plays at the plate is to have a coach or partner stand with a bat and a bucket of balls about 40 to 60 feet away and hit balls for us to field. This is the most realistic practice we can get besides actually taking throws from outfielders. We want our partner to hit balls off a bat is because the ball will react in a very similar way to a ball that is thrown from an outfielder.

It is important for the coach to change position and move around so we can simulate balls thrown from all areas of the field. They should also hit forehand and backhand balls, long hops, short hops, and in-between hops, and every type of ball possible, so that we have practice catching as many different types of balls as possible.

Another good time to practice this drill is during batting practice. Instead of shagging balls in the outfield and not working on any specific catching skills, we could put on our gear and field ground balls with the third or first baseman. Instead of fielding and throwing across the diamond, we should practice fielding the ball and then tagging a runner.

1, 2, 3 Double Play

The 1, 2, 3, double play gets its name from how it is officially scored in the scorebook. This is a play in which the bases are loaded and there is a ground ball hit to the pitcher. The pitcher will throw it to the catcher for the first out, and then the catcher will throw the ball to the first baseman for the second out.

This drill will start with the coach or partner standing in front of the pitcher's mound about 40 to 50 feet away with the catcher in his normal position, in foul territory behind home plate. Our partner will throw the ball to us and simulate a ball that has been hit back to the pitcher. We will then have to catch the throw, swipe our foot across home plate, and make a good throw to the first baseman.

To make the drill as realistic as possible, our coach should throw us balls that are hard to handle as well as good throws. This will prepare us to handle any throw a pitcher may make to us in a game. If the throw is so poor that we must leave home plate, our goal should be to make sure that we step on home plate and at least get that forced out.

Full Arm Fake and Look to 3B

Another variation of the 1, 2, 3 Double Play Drill that we should practice is adding a Full Arm Fake and then throwing to third base. This is practice for the situation in which we won't be able to finish the double play at first base. Instead of conceding that the play is over, we should full arm fake to first base and then look to third base. If the base runner has made too big a turn, we can then attempt to throw him out.

The only way that this play will ever work is if we have a believable full arm fake to first base, so we need to practice it just like any other skill. Once we catch the ball from our partner, we should go through the exact same footwork as the 1, 2, 3 Double Play, except that we should hold on to the ball and full arm fake to first base. After the full arm fake, we should throw the ball to the third baseman, who is standing on the base.

Chapter 30

Drills for Pass Balls/Wild Pitches

There are many different drills for receiving, blocking, and throwing to bases, but there aren't many different ways to practice fielding pass balls or wild pitches. That's OK, though! We don't need to have fancy drills to improve our skills, we just need to focus on practicing very deliberately.

We should start behind home plate on our knees in a good blocking position. This is because we are usually running balls down that we either weren't able to catch or didn't block. This will help us practice getting out of our blocking position quickly to retrieve balls. Our partner should throw a ball to the backstop and then act as the pitcher covering home plate. We will sprint to the ball, field it using the mechanics that we learned earlier in this book, and make a firm throw that is easy for our partner or the pitcher to handle.

Balls should be thrown all over the backstop, not just directly behind the catcher. We need to practice recovering balls that are thrown toward the first and third base dugouts as well as balls thrown directly behind us.

It is important to practice fielding pass balls and wild pitches in all sorts of weather conditions. When it is wet outside, we are going to slide differently on our shin guards than we will when the field is dry. Rainy days offer a great opportunity to practice this, and we should take advantage of them.

Another smart idea is to practice this with our pitching staff. They need the practice running from the mound, catching the throw, and applying the tag on the runner.

Chapter 31

Drills for Fielding Bunts

Similar to fielding pass balls and wild pitches, there aren't many out of the ordinary drills that help us improve fielding bunts. If we concentrate on the most important points of emphasis, we will find ourselves prepared to field bunts during a game.

We should practice fielding bunts starting from our primary and secondary stances. Our coach or partner will stand behind us in foul territory, where the umpire would stand, and roll balls for us to field. Balls should be rolled to all areas of the field–first base line, back to the pitcher, and down the third base line–at different speeds and distances. We should try to simulate every possible type of bunt, including balls that have come to a complete stop and balls that are still rolling while we field them. After we field the ball, we should concentrate on making a good throw that our infielder can easily handle.

Even though blocked third strikes aren't bunts, they are fielded the same way. That is why we should practice them at the same time we practice fielding bunts. To simulate a blocked third strike, we should start on our knees in a good blocking position and have our partner roll balls all over the field, including foul territory. If the ball is rolled into foul territory on the first base side, we should be loud and communicate to the first baseman that he should be standing in foul territory by screaming, "Outside, outside!"

Because fielding bunts are usually pressure plays, we should practice fielding them in pressure situations. Pressure plays can be simulated by having players bunt a thrown ball and then sprint to first base. This will also help our bunters get practice. We will now be forced to field the bunt and make a good throw before the runner touches first base. If we don't want to use actual base runners, we could simulate this situation using a stopwatch. The coach, or partner, should start the stopwatch whenever the ball is bunted or rolled. The catcher will field it and throw the ball to first base. When the ball impacts the first baseman's mitt, we should stop the stopwatch. A good goal is to make the play in less than four seconds, but as we get older and more skilled, we can decrease the time allowed to increase the difficulty of the drill.

While the majority of our throws will be thrown to first base, it is also important to practice fielding bunts and throwing to second base and third base, as well. If the batter makes a poor sacrifice bunt and we can field it and throw the lead runner out, we can completely change the momentum of the inning. These situations won't arise very often, but when they do we want to know that we are prepared to throw the lead runner out because we have practiced it.

Chapter 32

Summary

We have covered a lot of different things that catchers need to do well in order to have success and advance to the next level of baseball. Catchers have more skills to master than any other position player does, and that requires us to work harder, and smarter, than other players!

I hope that you will take the information in this book and apply it to your game so that you can reach your full potential. Baseball can be an extremely rewarding game, but it is also very challenging. Respect the game, work as hard as you can, and good things will happen! By reading this book, you have shown that you want to learn more about the most exciting position on the field. Now you must put in hours upon hours of hard work to hone your skills and master your craft. Don't ever let anyone tell you that you can't reach your goals!

If your goal is to play in the Big Leagues it will take a lot of hours of work and you will surely face adversity along the way. I encourage you to work as hard as you can every day and take advantage of each opportunity that is given to you. If you do that, you will be a success, whether you make it to the Big Leagues or not. Good luck!

Chapter 33

Catcher's Dictionary

Arm Side - The side of the plate relative to a pitcher's arm. Ex: A right-handed pitcher throwing inside to an RHH or outside to an LHH is throwing Arm Side. A left-handed pitcher throws Arm Side when he throws inside to an LHH, or away from an RHH.

Breaking Ball - A term used to describe either a curveball or a slider.

Bullpen - a) The practice mounds on the side of a field that pitchers use to get warmed up before going into the game. b) The act of a pitcher practicing pitching off the mound.

Crossed up - When the pitcher throws a different pitch than what the catcher signaled for.

Cut - When a pitch has movement away from the pitcher's arm side.

CATCHING-101

Five Hole - The gap between a catcher's legs when he goes down on his knees to block a pitch thrown in the dirt.

Fungo - A long, skinny baseball bat made for coaches to use during practice.

Glove Side - The side of the plate relative to a pitcher's non-throwing arm. Ex: A right-handed pitcher throwing away from an RHH, or inside to an LHH, is throwing Glove Side. A left-handed pitcher throws Glove Side when he is throwing inside to an RHH, or outside to an LHH.

Handcuffed - When a pitch is thrown in an awkward place (usually around the left knee) and the catcher doesn't know if he should catch the ball with his mitt up or down.

IBB - Intentional Base on Balls.

Intentional Walk - When you walk a batter on purpose so that you do not have to face him.

LHH - A left-handed hitter.

Off-Speed Pitch - Any pitch other than a fastball.

On The Same Page - When a catcher and pitcher are "on the same page," they are thinking alike. Ex: A pitcher and catcher are on the same page when they both want to throw the same pitch the majority of the time.

The Complete Guide for Baseball Catchers

Pop time - : The time it takes for a catcher to throw the ball to second base. The stopwatch is started when the pitch touches the catcher's mitt and stopped when the infielder catches the ball.

Primary Stance - : The stance that catchers use when there are no runners on base and less than two strikes.

Punch Out - : A strike out (more commonly when a batter strikes out looking).

RHH - : A right-handed hitter.

Run - : When a pitch has movement to the pitcher's arm side.

Secondary Stance - : The stance that catchers use when there are runners on base or there are two strikes on the hitter.

Side Work - : Another term used for a bullpen session.

Signal Stance - : The stance that catchers get into while they are relaying signals to the pitcher.

Slide Step - : When a pitcher doesn't lift his leg high off the ground but slides it along the dirt so that he is quicker delivering the pitch to home plate. This is done in an effort to help catchers throw base stealers out.

Strike Out Backwards - : When a batter strikes out looking.

CATCHING-101

Verbal - A word or phrase that acts as a signal.

CPSIA information can be obtained
at www.ICGtesting.com
Printed in the USA
FSHW011328180219
55754FS

9 781463 439613